Critical

Choices

in

Interviews

Conduct, Use, and
Research Role

INSTITUTE OF GOVERNMENTAL STUDIES

Eugene C. Lee, *Director*

The Institute of Governmental Studies was established in 1919 as the Bureau of Public Administration, and given its present name in 1962. One of the oldest research units in the University of California, the Institute conducts extensive and varied research and service programs in such fields as public policy, politics, urban-metropolitan problems, and public administration. The Institute focuses on issues confronting the Bay Area, California, and the nation.

The professional staff includes faculty members holding joint Institute and departmental appointments, research specialists, librarians, editors, and graduate students. In addition the Institute encourages policy-oriented research and writing efforts by a variety of faculty members and researchers not formally affiliated with the staff. The Institute is also host to visiting scholars from other parts of the United States and many foreign nations.

A prime resource in its endeavors is the Institute Library, with more than 380,000 documents, pamphlets, and periodicals relating primarily to government and public affairs. Holdings include a number of major special collections. The Library serves faculty and staff members, students, public officials, and other interested citizens.

The Institute also publishes books, monographs, bibliographies, periodicals, research reports, and reprints for a national audience. It issues the bimonthly Institute bulletin, the *Public Affairs Report,* dealing with problems in public policy; and the occasional publication, *California Data Brief,* which presents timely data on the state's social and economic development.

In addition, the Institute sponsors lectures, conferences, workshops and seminars that bring together faculty members, public officials, and other citizens. It administers the California Policy Seminar, a unique University-wide effort involving faculty and state government officials in a program of research on public policy issues confronting the state.

These programs and publications are intended to stimulate thought, research, and action by scholars, citizens, and public officials on significant governmental policies and social issues.

Harriet Nathan

Institute of Governmental Studies and
Regional Oral History Office, The Bancroft Library

Critical

Choices

in

Interviews

*Conduct, Use, and
Research Role*

INSTITUTE OF GOVERNMENTAL STUDIES
University of California, Berkeley ● 1986

Library of Congress Cataloging-in-Publication Data

Nathan, Harriet.
    Critical choices in interviews.

      Bibliography: p.
      1. Interviewing. 2. Oral communication. 3. Research.
I. Title.
P96.I54N38   1986   001.54'2   86-10523
ISBN 0-87772-309-5

Design: Carolyn S. Hughes

Contents

Notes   123

Illustrations

_____

Foreword

In her opening pages, Harriet Nathan quotes John Brady—"Questioning has always been the chief form of learning and satisfying curiosity"—a text she applies to the subject of her book. By analyzing different forms of inquiry, she brings to bear a lifetime of experience, thus "satisfying curiosity" respecting this critical feature of contemporary communication and investigation, i.e., the interview.

Her net is cast broadly in attempting to capture the common characteristics and principal differences among several kinds of questioning—survey research and polling, journalistic inquiry, scholarly research, and oral history. These seemingly disparate uses of the interview all pose issues of control and flexibility, ethics, and technique. Each of these themes is discussed with care and sophistication from the standpoint of the five types of participants in the interview process: interviewer, narrator, researcher, editor/publisher, and reader. "Interviews," she concludes, "are a virtually inexhaustible source of human understanding . . . a precious, renewable human resource."

Harriet Nathan has also been a rich resource, commencing with her student days at Berkeley in Journalism, when she was awarded Phi Beta Kappa honors in her junior year, while simultaneously serving as the first woman managing editor of the *Daily Californian,* the student newspaper. Her campus and community activities have also included research and writing for the late President Robert Gordon Sproul and for the University's Centennial publications, a distinguished record of activity with the Leagues of Women Voters of San Francisco, Berkeley, and California, including the Berkeley League presidency, and active participation in school district reorganization in

Alameda County. For many years she has served as a senior member of the staff of the Regional Oral History Office of The Bancroft Library and as Principal Editor of the publications program of the Institute of Governmental Studies. The experience and insights she has acquired in this varied and stimulating career—writer, researcher, oral historian, editor, participant observer—are all employed to great advantage in this study of the interview.

Wise, humane, and with a keen wit and high intellect, Harriet Nathan is a superb colleague whose editorial activities and advice have helped faculty and research associates, as well as hundreds of students, on this and other campuses. It is a privilege to publish this volume and, in so doing, to honor her record of service to the University.

Eugene C. Lee
Director

Preface

This comparative study of interviews is the product of a growing appreciation of interviews themselves, recognition of their variety, and awareness of their potential for benefit or harm. The writer's experience with interviews through work as an interviewer, editor, researcher, writer, and reader soon elevated interest to fascination. A closer look led to comparisons of style and purpose, and a tentative identification of such organizing principles as control, techniques, and ethics. These elements proved useful in distinguishing among critical choices needed to promote the optimum conduct and use of interviews, particularly in research.

Despite thoughtful literature on several types of interviews, there seems to be little if any systematic comparative analysis across a range of prototypes. Conversations with students, faculty members, and other users and interviewers suggested the need for such a comparative study as a way of presenting options, and banishing the ambiguity that dims the promise of effective interviews. Accepting the premise that interviews are valuable channels of communication, we find it worthwhile to cultivate and protect these channels. What others possess or suggest of fact, interpretation, perception, memory, and ideas can be elicited through interviews to enrich one's own store of information, understanding, and insight. The first step is to recognize the range of choices, to know what the choices may be, and to choose wisely.

Researchers in particular need to know the characteristics and quirks of each interview style; other interview participants and users have needs of their own. A major purpose of this analysis is to stimulate the thinking of students and researchers who are exploring the use of interviews, as well as experienced investigators, professors and teachers, journalists, survey researchers, policymakers, and citizens concerned with questions of public policy. Knowing how to think about, classify, analyze, and select interviews can help practitioners make critical choices about their own work and better evaluate the work of others.

To establish interviews on firmer ground is a sizeable challenge, one that proved appropriate within the University of California's Institute of Governmental Studies. For decades the Institute has produced carefully researched, edited, and verified publications, including several that featured scholarly research interviews. An additional stimulus for this paper was the 1977 conference on "Media Performance in Political Campaigns," funded by the Ford Foundation and cosponsored by the Institute; the Graduate School of Journalism at the University of California, Berkeley; the *California Journal;* and the Department of Communication, Stanford University. The issues, problems, and ideas vividly expressed there proved prophetic. Readers will note references to those discussions, based on the Institute's draft conference report. Further, the production of oral history interviews with the Regional Oral History Office of The Bancroft Library mirrored development in the field, and presented a rational format that offered comparisons with other kinds of interviews.

Research began with a literature survey based primarily on library collections at the University of California, Berkeley. These included publications and materials found in the Institute and its Library, in the University's Main Library, and in that of the Graduate School of Journalism. Other sources were documents, books, and interviews produced and collected by the Regional Oral History Office of The Bancroft Library and the Survey Research Center Library. These readings stimulated development of the concepts and, along with current newspapers and journals, as well as items from Berkeley's used-book stores, provided many of the illustrative examples. The writer also conducted a number of interviews and conversations for this study. At the draft-reviewing stage, expert readers generously contributed clippings and examples from their own reading and experience.

The method of inquiry was to examine the conduct and use of interviews, focusing on the four major kinds identified for study—survey research and polling, journalistic, scholarly research, and oral history. The analysis also addressed theoretical principles defined as the control and flexibility exercised in the conduct of interviews, the ethics, and the techniques that govern the functions of each type of interview. In addition, it dealt with such questions as whether one should conduct and use interviews in given contexts, and what the choices may be.

The roles of major participants in the process were designated and examined, i.e., interviewer, narrator, researcher, editor, and final user. Selected examples showed interviews in action, as well as commentary and interpretation of the politics of the interviews, or who gets what out of the transaction.

These concepts, theories, and selected examples of interviews and comments are intended to demystify interviews by analyzing their elements. Once the elements are understood the deluge of interviews becomes less overwhelming, and recognition of types becomes possible. When the types are sorted out and the principles of conduct and use understood, one can recognize options and choices to use or discard opportunities with some confidence.

The inattentive person in the world of interviews, our world, is like the unsophisticated traveler of an earlier era. We now smile at the outdated complaints that all foreigners looked alike. Only when the traveler got to know individuals did they become recognizable and real persons. For many of us, interviews are still like inhabitants of an enormous and confusing foreign place; interested but intimidated, we take a hasty glance at the mass and assume that they are all alike. But when we recognize their individuality and their component elements, think about them, and understand them, we soon learn their distinctions as well as their rich and rewarding variety.

Harriet Nathan

Acknowledgments

As many have noted, the Berkeley campus of the University of California (UCB) has a rich concentration of research facilities and libraries, as well as persons with specialized and expert knowledge. In addition, the area attracts a host of non-campus experts.

I am grateful for the generous help of many faculty and staff members, librarians, students, colleagues, and other narrators both on and off-campus. Only a few can be thanked here. Eugene C. Lee, director of the Institute of Governmental Studies recognized the possibilities in a study that would investigate the role of interviews in research. He encouraged the venture, and provided support for research and writing. Essential help was also given by those who read and commented on earlier drafts, and in several cases offered material of their own.

Faculty members in various settings provided opportunities to develop and test ideas. These included Todd R. La Porte, IGS associate director, who arranged for me to discuss interviewing with his political science classes at Berkeley; Peggy Webb whose invitation to lead seminars on interviewing in journalism and English classes at Mills College served as the initial springboard for this paper; and Verneice Thompson, dean of the Institute of Clinical Social Work, through a seminar discussion with Ph.D. candidates on the use of interviews in research. At Berkeley's Graduate School of Journalism, Ben H. Bagdikian, now dean, provided a unique opportunity to hear members of his class discuss their views on specific cases in journalistic ethics. He was also a reader and generous contributor of material from his own experience.

Others who served as readers and/or contributors of interviews, consultation, and additional material have my particular thanks. They include Dorothy C. Tompkins, emeritus bibliographer at IGS, for her valuable clippings; Dean Emeritus Edwin R. Bayley and faculty member Lacey Fosburgh of the Berkeley Graduate School of Journalism (Fosburgh also permitted me to paraphrase her own unpublished material); Mervin D. Field of The Field Institute; Lynn Wood, assistant director of the Teaching Innovation and Evaluation Services (TIES), UCB; Beatrice M. Bain, coordinator, Agriculture and Natural Resources, UCB; Mary Ellen Leary, journalist and author; and Ed Salzman, editor and publisher (some of whose dissenting views are here acknowledged).

Many Institute colleagues have been generous with help, support, and instruction. To mention two: Assistant Director Stanley Scott, researcher, writer, and prime editorial mentor, who also provided interviews and significant consultation; and Senior Editor Janet Isadore-Barreca, editor's editor, whose editorial judgment and skill proved invaluable. Willa K. Baum, division head, Regional Oral History Office (ROHO) of The Bancroft Library, provided staff seminars, her own publications and those of others, leadership in the field, and valuable advice to me as an oral history interviewer/editor for two decades. Other interviewer/editor colleagues at ROHO offered useful counsel and ideas on many occasions. These expert practitioners included Gabrielle Morris, Malca Chall, Sarah Sharp, Julie Shearer, Amelia (Chita) Fry, Suzanne Riess, Anne H. Brower, Ruth Teiser, the late Catherine Harroun, Elaine Dorfman, Ann Lage, Eleanor Glaser, Judith Dunning, and the late Catherine Scholten. The writer acknowledges, however, that this discussion may not always agree with the views of these experienced, strong-minded, thoughtful, and skilled oral history interviewers and editors.

Several UCB librarians were particularly helpful. These included Jack Leister, IGS head librarian, and members of his staff; Ilona Einowski, data archivist at the State Data Program, Survey Research Center; and David Brown, formerly at the Library of the Graduate School of Journalism.

It is a pleasure to thank the resourceful and talented professionals at IGS whose teamwork produced this volume: Carolyn S. Hughes, artist and designer; Pat Ramirez, publications coordinator; Janice McCrear, data processing assistant; Maria Wolf, assistant editor; and Kim Denison, bibliographer. I am also proud to claim as family members and critical readers Elinor Bernal, bilingual teacher and editor; Ann Nathan Johnson, recreational therapist and college teacher; and Edward Nathan, licensed clinical social worker and foundation executive. They knew how to identify many points that needed clarification, and to balance these discoveries by finding and praising the better ones. Finally, I am grateful to Byron Coleman, whose lively interest spurred the project to completion.

For the interest, stimulus, and support of colleagues and other professionals, friends, and family members, I am deeply grateful. The views expressed are mine, not those of the the Institute or the University, and any errors of fact or interpretation are my own.

I

Participants, Interests, and Process

INTRODUCTION

Two people talk to each other, but not in the give-and-take of conversation. One asks questions and the other answers. This is an interview, a form of communication and information-gathering whose origins lie in the beginnings of human gesture and speech. The interviewer questions the narrator because the latter knows, remembers, or understands information the interviewer wants or needs to hear. John Brady noted in a history of "the interview" that "Questioning has always been the chief form of learning and satisfying curiosity . . . "[1]

What is said in interviews may then be trusted to memory, recorded by the reporter's pencil and paper, stored on a cassette tape or by the computer's keys. Whether typed, retaped, transcribed, compiled, or filed and forgotten, interviews tend to join a flow that has become a flood. The current pervasiveness of interviews has become so familiar that it may well be "an unappreciated innovation of modern times,"[2] in both quantity and variety.

Virtually every newspaper offers interview quotes or reports the findings of polls and surveys. Books and journals incorporate interviews and the accounts they generate. Applicants for writing jobs often have to demonstrate knowledge of interviewing. In short, interviews are all too familiar, but their numbers do not guarantee either our understanding or recognition of their variety.

Each interview has a particular style, and recognizable characteristics. Some are free-wheeling, even antagonistic and combative; others standardized, formal, and bland. Still others may be reflective and cooperative in tone, revealing sympathetic rapport between interviewer and narrator. Some interviews take the form of brief exchanges with hundreds of respondents; and still others require a score or more extended sessions with one individual. Each has its own particular value, and arouses specific expectations.

At times, however, expectations may be unrealistic and confused, so that a user criticizes one type of interview (for example, scholarly research) because it lacks the character of another type (for example, journalistic). Another example: some oral history interviews may be challenged as not factual, although the information may have been checked with other sources, and the verification incorporated for reference. Or a user may treat a quote from a journalistic interview as if it were revealed truth, although it was merely one person's reported statement that signaled the need for verification.

It is remarkable that such a simple event, with one person asking questions and one answering, can produce such wide-ranging experiences. To call all these events and products "interviews" is necessary but not sufficient identification; it is a kind of shorthand that leads easily to misunderstandings and unjustified expectations. The solution is to define further, to find and choose the right modifier that signifies the strengths, weaknesses, and appropriate conduct and use of each kind of interview. The goal of this study is to clarify choices in interviews to foster their optimum conduct and use. The central problem is vagueness; the solution will lie in specificity.

Why Interview Types Need to Be Specific

As we distinguish among and define types of interviews, we need to
1. identify and clarify what can be expected in the conduct and use of each type and specify what choices are appropriate and under what circumstances, with particular attention to the needs of researchers;
2. encourage consensus on ground rules for the conduct and use of each major type of interview;
3. promote the interests of participants and users, and minimize adverse or destructive consequences;
4. facilitate improved performance in research, through choice of the most effective and efficient interview type for each job;
5. provide appropriate levels of confidence in the use of interview material; and
6. further the effective use of all interview types as an extraordinary human resource. What individuals know and can talk about is a resource that is renewed with each successive generation, one that should be used wisely and well.

Risks of misuse are rooted in ignorance or lack of planning, e.g., failure to ask specific questions about interview conduct or purpose, misplaced trust, inappropriate confidence in accuracy or reliability, unsuitable expectations on the part of participants or users, and disappointing yields of usable material in return for invested time, effort, and money.

These risks, however, can be minimized by knowledge and forethought, and transformed into positive, informed choices. The strategy lies in recognizing and selecting the right interview for the purpose; the tactics emerge in the conduct and use of each interview style in its most appropriate context.

Who Needs to Know

Those involved in teaching, learning, and doing research—faculty members, graduate and undergraduate students, advisors, and researchers—urgently need to judge the reliability of interviews and the advisability of their use. This is true in the process of daily learning, teaching, reading, and writing, and assumes a sharp necessity in the writing of research proposals. Researchers must be realistic about using interviews conducted by others, and also training their own interviewers and maintaining quality control. Researchers must decide, for example, whether research schedules should comprise survey interviews, journalistic interviews designed to challenge key informants, or oral history interviews. They must be able to assess costs and benefits of each option.

For those outside of academia, public figures and other prominent persons choose whether or not to talk to journalists. Would it be better to risk possible confrontation in a journalistic interview to reach the widest or most significant audience? Would scholarly research interviews or a full-scale oral history memoir assure maximum control as well as impact? Is time a factor? What are the individual's expectations in each case?

Those who are relatively unaccustomed to the spotlight—survivors of a disaster, for example—may also face would-be interviewers. What questions should they ask the questioners? What protections or agreements should be established before the narrators face the first question?

Anyone seeking information on public issues faces a flood of survey and polling reports, and a host of other interviews. How does one evaluate these reports? What should be accepted, questioned, or rejected?

Finally, many kinds of interviewing have become so highly specialized that expertise in one type does not imply expertise in all. In the long run, we are all consumers, and often participants, linked in a chain of mutual expectations, concerns, and responsibilities.

THE CHAIN OF ELEMENTS AND TYPES

The components of this study are summarized in the preface and developed in subsequent chapters, but it may be useful to state them here to observe how one concept leads to another. If we accept the notion of a politics of interviews, it is appropriate to keep in mind the question of whose interests are served in each case and each interview type. The play of interests points up the characteristics that help us differentiate among survey research and polling, journalistic, scholarly research, and oral history interviews. The characteristics in turn have been shaped by such governing principles as control and flexibility, techniques, and ethics.

The theoretical concepts grew from politics-related questions, e.g., "who controls this interview: the interviewer or the narrator?" Along the spectrum of control, as we will see, the interviewer exerts greatest control in survey research; the narrator, in oral history. Other types and sub-types have found their own locations on the spectrum. Concepts of ethics and techniques emerged from the question, "What is appropriate in this kind of interview?" The answer was different for each type. To ask "How are the interests of participants and users protected?" led again to analysis of how one learns what to expect of the ethics and techniques of each interview type.

Participants and users, actors with interests in the conduct and use of interviews, assume their roles as interviewer, narrator, researcher, editor/publisher, and final reader with interests that are sometimes shared and sometimes in conflict. Further, roles can overlap, as when the researcher becomes an interviewer to conduct his or her own interviews, or uses interviews that have been conducted under other auspices and in various styles. At times, many become narrators, and virtually everyone is a reader and ultimate user. Finally, interviews remain subject to the same strictures as all other modes of research: their statements must be checked and verified by use of other sources.

Like other theories, our notions of elements and types need the test of real-world performance. One test is to apply them to examples of interview conduct and use to see whether they illuminate the problems encountered or help us understand the successes, failures, and dilemmas our colleagues experience. To this end, the text includes more than 50 examples, both good and bad, of interview experiences, comments, and discussions by interviewers, narrators, editors, researchers, and sometimes bemused observers.

Before turning to a closer consideration of interview types, a word may be in order. Americans tend to be at ease with the spoken word; we are verbal, and many of us speak more easily and readily than we write. We are familiar with interviews, and recognize when one person tries to elicit information from another. (This interview is a familiar experience of childhood: "Where did you go?" "Out." "What did you do?" "Nothing.") Because we know and use interviews easily, to observe and recognize different types may simply be to acknowledge familiar experiences and use them in a somewhat different way.

FOUR MAJOR INTERVIEW TYPES: SOME DESCRIPTIONS

As we have seen, the four selected interview types considered here are survey research and polling, journalistic, scholarly research, and oral history.

Further discussion appears in chapters II, III, and IV. Brief introductions are appropriate here.

1. Survey research and its sub-type, opinion polling, include canvassing a sample population by use of a question schedule with fixed sequence and wording of questions. The objective is to eliminate bias due to variations in questions, or introduced by the interviewers' attitudes. Respondents remain anonymous.

2. In the journalistic interview, in common with others, the interviewer seeks information from a narrator by asking questions and getting answers. Special characteristics include emphasis on what is newsworthy, timely, and unique, often underscored by the importance of the narrator's name. Source attribution or protection of anonymity is often an issue to be discussed and sometimes fought over in a journalistic interview. The tightest of timetables and the most onerous of deadline pressures usually apply to journalistic interviews, although a longer time-span may be allowed when the product is destined for journals or books.

3. The scholarly research interview is usually designed for use in an academic research project. This interview often operates under longer-term deadlines. Some form of review by the narrator and approval of the interview material and interpretations frequently occurs and the narrator's own name is usually used.

4. The oral history interview may be primarily biographical or topic-oriented. In the biographical memoir, the interviewer's questions are usually approved by the narrator, who has considerable freedom about answering questions or choosing other topics. The narrator approves the final draft. As their name suggests, the sub-category of topic-oriented oral history interviews tend to focus on and be restricted to selected topics or events around which a series of shorter interviews is organized. The narrator has full control of the contents of the final draft, but is not normally free to include extraneous material.

Oral histories are deposited in research libraries or other collections such as those of historical societies and museums, where they can be preserved, maintained, and administered for the use of future researchers. As a rule, production deadlines are relatively unimportant for oral histories.

Additional Types and the Byline Analogy

The four types noted above do not comprise an all-inclusive list. Other kinds of interviews abound, including some hybrids that share characteristics of more than one of the four types selected here. For example, the journalistic "man in the street" interviews may suggest a sense of public opinion. They are neither typical journalistic interviews nor opinion polls, although they include elements of each. Journalists sometimes also do biographical interviews that share some aspects of oral history interviews, but differ in end results and uses.

6

In addition, a newspaper column, feature story, or news story that carries a "byline" identifying the writer is analogous to some types of interviews. Interviews present quotations or paraphrases of a narrator's words (with the exception of survey interviews that record only the gist of the response of an anonymous narrator). Interviews take on the identity of the narrator in the same way byline articles do for the writer; each becomes part of that person's observable record. The writer/word connections become significant when the reader makes decisions and choices about which writer to read, believe, and trust just as interviews influence the reader's perceptions of the narrator.

Significance of Clues

The researcher/user needs to identify the interview type as a first step in evaluating the interview as a data source, i.e., judging how good a given interview transcript may be for a particular purpose. For example, a journalistic interview can provide clues, information, and insights, but not statistically reliable survey data; only formal surveys and structured polling interviews can serve that purpose. Oral history interviews can and do supply the name of the narrator or the full statement of a quote, whereas survey interviews preserve anonymity. In the journalistic interview, the narrator typically does not review and correct direct quotes unless the interviewer offers that option. In contrast, this happens often with scholarly research interviews, and oral history interviews typically involve review and correction of attributed comments.

The survey research or polling interview is a means to an end. It provides elements in an array of statistical data destined for conversion into usable information. The journalistic interview can be an end in itself, as the principal basis of a column or a news or feature story, used as background information, or as one component among a number of sources. Thus a journalistic interview may either be the story, or contribute to the immediate construction of one.

A scholarly research interview may also comprise the whole story, be an integral part of it, or simply contribute background for further work. Its significance usually involves a longer-term perspective. The oral history interview's function is to contribute to the historical record, capturing primary material for later use by researchers. Thus the oral history interview is not the final product, but a means of preserving information for the future.

Choices may be influenced by knowing who controlled the conduct of an interview and the way it was written, transcribed, and/or published, as well as what agreements were made between interviewer and narrator. The researcher also needs to know whose interests were involved and which prevailed; what ethical principles were applied; and how the editor/publisher functioned. These are concerns that bear on the interests of all those involved: the interviewer, the narrator, the editor/publisher, the researcher, and the ultimate reader/user.

THREE PRINCIPLES:
HOW CIRCUMSTANCES ALTER CASES

We have seen how timing, deadlines, purposes, and uses vary with the type of interview These elements suggest why and how interviews function as they do, but a theoretical framework is needed to help explain the essential nature of each type. Three principles can provide a useful approach: control and flexibility, ethics, and techniques. These are involved in all interviews, but take different forms for each type.

1. In a two-person interview, one or the other participant exercises control, or both share it. Chapter II develops this idea, and examines how control and flexibility work for each interview type.

2. As in all human relationships, the ethics of behavior is an underlying consideration, honored, distorted, abused or ignored. The relativity of ethical concepts means that certain expectations and promises may be acceptable in the conduct and use of one interview type, but less so or not at all in another. One needs to ask to what extent ethics is type-specific, and whether certain over-arching ethical principles also apply universally (see Chapter III).

3. The nuts and bolts of techniques used to produce each type of interview vary from one type to another. Techniques shape the conduct and use of interviews and are adapted to the needs of the occasion. With this variety, however, we find consistent concepts that underlie technique (see Chapter IV).

Chapters V and VI go beyond the three organizing principles. As noted below, Chapter V focuses on editors and publishers, whose role in connection with interviews is seldom fully recognized, yet who exercise the power of entrepreneurs and gatekeepers. These players often assign interviews, and determine whether or in what form they will be published.

Chapter VI brings the discussion full circle to basic questions of whether to conduct or use interviews, and if so, why, and in what circumstances. Evaluation of options and of the special strengths and weaknesses of each type of interview, plus the availability of alternative sources of information, should help guide informed choices.

FIVE PARTICIPANTS AND USERS

The two central participants are the interviewer who asks questions, and the narrator who answers. The latter is sometimes referred to as "interviewee" or "respondent." "Interviewee," however, seems too passive, connoting one *to whom* something is done. The writer therefore chose "narrator" because it is active and thus a closer parallel to "interviewer." In survey research and polling, however, where the range of response is limited, the more restricted term—"respondent"—is often employed. It is used here where appropriate.

The interviewer, who conducts the interview, is usually the originator and prime mover. The interviewer is often a professional, sometimes acting on his or her own behalf, on other occasions as the representative of an employer or one who will purchase the interview as a product. The interviewer is the one who "picks the lock" of the narrator's information—as journalist Lacey Fosburgh has phrased it—so that the narrator can recognize and reveal material that otherwise might remain inaccessible.

The narrator, the essential second person in an interview, may be a leader or an experienced and knowledgeable observer. On the other hand, the narrator may have no special expertise or knowledge, but fall into a survey research sample, a "man on the street" asked for impressions, or an "innocent bystander," a disaster victim or survivor, stunned and tearful, unprepared for an onslaught of questions. In short, the narrator may be an expert, a public figure, one of the leadership elite in various fields, or a private or obscure person, or possibly a member of a community or group about whom information is being collected.

We have already touched on the concerns of the researcher, the third person in the ad hoc crew, who has a more complex function, often serving as principal investigator or employer. He or she may design interview projects, supervise interviewers or conduct the sessions personally, and edit and submit the interviews for publication. This job includes both conducting and using interviews. Using interviews conducted by others, and including those not necessarily intended for research, the researcher has a familiar but sometimes difficult role. The abundance of interview material can be a bonanza of information and insight, or a crushing avalanche. The responsibilities of the researcher are to recognize interview types, select and evaluate data, watch for clues on accuracy and reliability, and interpret information.[3]

The fourth participant is the editor/publisher, who often makes assignments and also acts as gatekeeper, controlling final presentation or publication, and deciding whether or not to publish. Within the editor/publisher group, of course, interests and needs can differ. The survey research firm or polling interviewer aims at eliminating bias in both interviewing and reporting, whereas the journalistic editor or publisher wants above all to get a good story first, with interesting and colorful detail. The scholarly editor needs relevant and reliable information and perhaps repeated access to the narrator. In oral history, the editor and interviewer are often the same person, whose primary interest is to encourage and facilitate the narrator's fullest response and to help make the final transcripts as clear and usable as possible. This is the only editor whose work does not relate to publication.

Finally, the reader is the ultimate consumer who may use interview material or the research it supports, looking for clues that could reveal facts, lead to interpretations, or provide illuminations.[4] The reader thus queues up at the end of the line. In theory all these people—interviewer, narrator, researcher, editor—are at work to publish the material so he or she can read it. Logically, the reader's interests should be paramount, yet that same reader is lost in a sea of unorganized and often unidentified information and left with but one choice: to accept the interview as valid or to reject it. That turns out to be no small share of power.

With this power, the reader remains a presence whose role and interests are implied, but not examined in detail here. The reader who waits for the interview does well to be aware of the many hands the interview experiences. These include the review and approval of the oral history narrator; editing and categorizing by survey research and polling analysts; writing and rewriting by the journalist-interviewer and editor; and selection and interpretation by the researcher, as well as the cutting, headline writing, and all the processing visited on written materials.

Through this treatment the interview may emerge relatively unscathed. On other occasions, it may resemble the original event to the same extent that a plate of sushi resembles a full-grown tuna. Nevertheless, both sushi and processed interview can have their uses, often providing nourishment in a form more convenient and useful than the sometimes unwieldy original. As long as the reader understands the nature and extent of the processing, he or she is free to be as skeptical or accepting as judgment permits.

Since the various roles listed above are distinctive, the interests involved can differ. The interviewer or questioner sees the interview as a means of obtaining information or creating a record. To the narrator or answerer, an interview provides a chance to be heard. The editor and/or publisher find opportunities to exercise choice and authority on the use of interview material, or over writings based on interviews. The researcher looks for viewpoints and opinions, factual information or at least clues, and leads to other sources. The ultimate reader may find enlightenment and insight in the transcribed or published account.

Admittedly these categories of participants and users may be too neat, too mutually exclusive. A researcher, for example, may also conduct interviews, and often uses interview material from many sources. A narrator also often reads interviews given by others. Further, virtually every literate person reads interviews, or material based on interviews, and in addition is likely to be interviewed. Interviews and their outreach are inescapable.

INTERVIEWS, RESEARCH, AND THE PRINT MEDIA

In its most basic form each interview is an exchange between two persons talking face-to-face, or alternatively on the phone. The number is two and only two. As interviewers know, the added presence of one person or more alters the relationship between interviewer and narrator. When three or more are present, an interview becomes a discussion or performance, changing the quality of rapport as well as the outcome of the session. At times two interviewers may seem desirable: when a skilled interview team can function almost as one, or when a second interviewer may be needed to provide substantiation.[5] Despite a few such exceptions, this discussion focuses on the two essential participants and excludes any others.

Even an absent audience is significant. In the one-to-one interviews examined here, microphones are connected only to the interviewer's cassette recorder. The setting excludes broadcasting devices, cameras, clusters of listeners, of questioners, or juries. The interviews considered here are not press conferences, media events, entertainments, or part of legal or religious procedures. They are not employment or eligibility interviews, or exchanges between client and therapist. While all of these and many others are significant types of interviews, their purposes, intent, and methodologies are different from those in this study, and extend beyond its scope. These two-person interviews have one major aim: to elicit information from the narrator.

Neither television nor radio interviews are included even though many people tune in on those conducted by Barbara Walters, Bill Moyers, Robert MacNeil, Jim Lehrer, or local newscasters. This study focuses on interviews whose results reach researchers and others largely through print media. A few words of explanation may be useful.

Television and radio interviews can be interesting and informative, but are generically different from those appearing in print. Non-print interviews have serious drawbacks related to reviewing, checking details and verbatim quotes, repeated consultations, and ease of reference. Hard copy still appears to be the preference of most researchers.

It is of course possible to tape one's own copy of a televised or broadcast interview, or in some cases to obtain transcripts, particularly if the program is on public radio or TV. Nonetheless, references to transcripts or texts of radio and TV interviews are typically not found in the library literature.[6]

The electronic media and the volume of interview material they process should not, however, be summarily dismissed. They may well be potentially useful sources. In the future more transcripts may be issued, and audio and video tapes may become more usable as playback and printout technology becomes cheaper and more widely available. Researchers may choose to record more interview programs on their own video cassette recorders. Increased ease in playing and replaying the tapes would permit researchers to take notes, select excerpts, or make verbatim transcripts as needed.

The "show biz" aspect of radio and TV is another, and probably more important, difference. The awareness of an audience transforms the reality of an interview in many ways.

The printed interview is directed to the reading audience. The broadcast audience watches and listens for the story, usually but not always expecting some level of entertainment, drama, or at least diversion. While such an audience need not be less intellectually inclined than the reading audience, watching the television may not aid critical thinking and research. Everette E. Dennis sees the relative emphasis this way: "Broadcasters are storytellers, newspapers are fact gathers and organizers of information, and news magazines are kind of a hybrid of both."[7] In Frances Fitzgerald's words, "reading above all . . . encourages critical thinking."[8]

SOME DEFINITIONS

This study does not offer guidelines or check lists for interviews. Instead, as suggested earlier, it proposes comparisons and theories, and invites analysis as a step toward making critical choices in the conduct and use of interviews. In the formulation of Harlan Cleveland (writing on a different subject), we seek "wisdom" in the conduct and use of interviews. His thinking includes the definition of "key words": data, information, knowledge, and wisdom; these terms can also designate the steps toward our goal.

First comes the selecting, refining, and organizing of *data* (facts, elements) related to interview types to produce *information.* Cleveland saw information as a semifinished product that becomes *knowledge* only after it is put to use in one's mind. The "integrated knowledge, information made super-useful by theory" relates "bits and fields of knowledge to each other," thus producing wisdom, and the ability to "use the knowledge to do something."[9] We seek to conduct and use interviews and to make critical choices with the wisdom that brings optimum results.

This study also uses key words, mostly familiar terms that mean something specific here.

1. *Control and flexibility* comprise one of the principles that defines interview types. Control here means the power to shape the conduct, use, reporting, and presentation of the interview. (Both terms apply here to the activities of the most immediate participants: the interviewer and the narrator.)

Control by the interviewer means guiding the technique (see below). It includes exercising the power to shape, articulate, and place questions in sequence (as for survey research and polling), to choose which portions of the interview will be emphasized, included, or deleted in the write-up, and with what comment and interpretation. Control by the narrator includes choosing which questions to answer and how, substituting more acceptable questions for those offered by the interviewer, and negotiating special treatment, such as anonymity.

Flexibility is the power to change direction as opportunity arises, or to make other spontaneous changes in the conduct of the interview. Control indicates who is in charge and suggests that power can be held by one participant or the other, or shared in varying proportions.

2. The *editor* is a supervisor, decisionmaker, and gatekeeper. Depending on the interview type, the editor can act at the beginning of the interview process, making assignments and directing content and conduct. After the interview, the editor can judge the quality and reliability of the interview material, determine emphasis, choose the lead, cut or require rewrite, postpone, or decline publication. Anticipation of "what the editor wants" can haunt the two-person interview with an invisible third presence.

3. *Ethics* is one of the three major principles that establish the nature of each interview style. Ethics involves standards and propriety, trust, and responsibility; no two interview styles require exactly the same attitudes and

behavior. An oral history interviewer does not divulge comments made during an interview; only the transcript, approved by the narrator, does that. A survey research interviewer protects the anonymity of the respondent. On the other hand, a journalistic interview faces no such ethical restraints unless they are specifically negotiated beforehand.

4. The *interview* in this study consists of questions and answers designed to produce information. The interviewer questions and the narrator answers.

5. The designated *interview styles* or *prototypes* are four: survey research and polling, journalistic, scholarly research, and oral history interviews. They serve as tools for analysis because their characteristics are consistent and distinguishable and permit comparison and contrast.

6. The *interviewer* is the participant who asks the questions and who may also write about the interview for publication, as in the journalistic and the scholarly research interviews. The same person may act in more than one capacity, as an interviewer who is also a researcher, and an ultimate user/reader as well.

7. The *journalistic interview,* a designated prototype, is customarily conducted with the intent of publication in a newspaper or other element of the print media, or as background to support and inform future publication. Its characteristic qualities are shaped by orientation toward what is newsworthy, and by the play of designated principles (i.e., control and flexibility, ethics, and techniques).

8. The *narrator* is the participant who answers the interviewer's questions, and is a partner in the two-person interview enterprise. In some contexts, the answerer is sometimes called "interviewee," "respondent," or "subject." This study uses narrator rather than interviewee to indicate that the answerer is not a passive figure, but one whose active role varies significantly from one interview type to another. Respondent and its use are defined below. Subject can be used to designate the answerer who is being questioned in a research project, often in a medical context. This highly specialized use is not explored here.

9. The *oral history interview* is a designated prototype, and is intended to capture and preserve material that would otherwise be lost. It is tape-recorded and often transcribed, conducted under specified conditions of narrator review and control in preparation for deposit in a research library, historical society collection, or other facility where it can be administered and made available for research use.

10. A *participant* is one who plays a role in the conduct, preparation, and use of interviews. The interviewer, narrator, editor, researcher, and ultimate reader/user are all participants.

11. A *principle,* or "essential element or quality that produces a specific effect,"[10] is one of three major elements this study identifies as shaping the characteristics of each interview prototype. The three principles are control and flexibility, ethics, and technique. If, for example, an interview were to be conducted and used according to the principles that shape a journalistic inter-

view, regardless of what it might be called, it would still be a journalistic interview.

12. The *publisher* of printed materials is considered here in relation to the editor. The publisher does not usually have the same hands-on relationship to the printed interview or story, but carries decisionmaking weight often by virtue of financial clout. The publisher and editor in some settings may be the same person. If not, the publisher's policy decisions may or may not be agreeable to the editor.

13. The *researcher* is one who relates to interviews in two ways. He or she may use interviews conducted by others; and also may conduct or authorize interviews to provide material for a project and eventual publication. The interests of the researcher provide a major stimulus for this study. The researcher who understands the elements of interviews, their styles, and their governing principles will know how to make critical choices and gain optimum benefits.

14. A *respondent* (see 8 above) is one who answers the interviewer's questions under certain restrictive conditions. In survey research and polling interviews, which are controlled by the interviewer, the respondent may answer the questions but may not digress in any significant way. The respondent must produce answers that fit predetermined categories in order to produce data. The respondent is and remains anonymous.

15. A *scholarly research interview,* one of the four designated prototypes, is conducted to produce background and publishable material, usually in an academic or other scholarly treatment. Characteristics are more fully discussed below, but it is worth noting that narrators usually are given the courtesy of reviewing the material attributed to them, and checking both fact and interpretation as presented.

16. A *survey research and polling interview,* one of the four designated prototypes, is conducted under rigorous rules designed to produce material that can be expressed in statistics through comparable categories. (See respondent, 14 above.)

17. *Technique,* or the ways the work gets done, is one of the principles that defines interview styles. It consists of procedures for planning, conducting, and using interviews. Elements include, e.g., variations in the interviewer's preparation, wording, kinds, and sequence of questions, tones and attitudes, methods of answering, uses of silence, the ways the interview is written for publication, as well as the use of tools such as computers, tape recorders, pencil and paper. Appropriateness is significant in the choice and use of techniques.

SUMMARY

An interview is a simple event: two people talk in question and answer. Complications arise when the variety and numbers of interviews increase and more people become involved without fully understanding what is happening, what to require, or what to expect. Further, as in all human relationships, promises, expectations, contests for control, and ethical considerations come into play, whether or not they are recognized.

This study argues that there is no such thing as "an interview," in either theory or practice. To convey substantial meaning, "interview" requires a modifier: survey research and polling, journalistic, scholarly research, or oral history. These four prototypes of interview styles are designated; they are by no means inclusive and remain subject to the reader's question, challenge, and modification. Participants in and users of all interview styles are identified here, and their interests noted; they are the interviewer, narrator, researcher, editor/publisher, and final reader/user. This study also formulates three generating principles that create interview types; the principles are control and flexibility, ethics, and technique.

Having proposed prototypes, participants, and principles, the discussion deals with both theory and conclusions, illustrated by examples that present the actual practices and problems of interview conduct and use. The combination of theory and practice in this and subsequent chapters is designed to remind readers of what they already know about interviews and perhaps suggest new ways of analyzing and thinking about them, in preparation for making critical decisions and choices about conduct and use, and with luck increasing enjoyment of the process.

We turn now to Chapter II and the first principle: control and flexibility, which soon points out who is in charge and why.

II

Control and Flexibility:
Who Is in Charge and Why

THE POLITICS OF INTERVIEWS

Each interviewer and each narrator has some interest to protect or advance through competition or cooperation. These concerns create the politics of interviews, a concept that implies the exercise of control. Control, with its option of flexibility, is the first governing principle in the conduct and use of interviews. At each step—preparation, conduct, write-up, and use of interviews—control relates to who does what and why.

Later discussion of two additional principles, ethics and techniques, will deal respectively with moral overtones of right and wrong and with procedures that determine how the work gets done. Important as they are, they take second place to control. It is the presence or absence of contest between interviewer and narrator and the ways that contest is resolved that most clearly reveal the nature of each session.

Portraying A Continuum of Control

Control can be seen as a continuum that extends from one pole (portrayed on the left in Chart 1) representing maximum control by the interviewer, to the other pole (on the right) representing maximum control by the narrator. For purposes of discussion, each of the four designated major interview types can occupy an area on the continuum. Survey research and polling interviews exemplify the greatest interviewer control, and appear farthest to the left on the chart. In journalistic interviews, while the narrator sometimes challenges the control exercised by the interviewer, the latter nevertheless typically guides the proceedings and write-up. Consequently journalistic interviews appear between survey research and the center position in the chart.

The scholarly interview often gives the narrator the power to review and thus exert substantial control. This interview type is placed to the right of the center position, where the narrator's control is seen to outweigh that of the interviewer. The oral history interview is placed farthest to the right, signifying maximum narrator control. Here the narrator often, but not always, controls much of the interview's conduct, content, and disposition.

CHART 1

Locating Control: Interview Types Placed on a Continuum

1	2	3	4
A		B	C

Interview Type	Location of Control
1: Survey research and polling	A: Maximum control by the interviewer
2: Journalistic	B: Control shared equally
3: Scholarly research	C: Maximum control by the narrator
4: Oral history	

To place these four major interview types on the chart is a useful first step in analysis, but one that also calls for a caveat. Many variations cluster around each interview type. Some borrow the characteristics of more than one main type. The profile, "conversations with . . ." or "dialogues with . . ." may include aspects of journalism as well as oral history; and other examples range from man-on-the-street columns to many kinds of biographical interviews. Further, interviews within the same type can vary substantially, influenced by factors that include the character, intellect, emotions, and preferences of the participants. Interviews are sometimes filled with conflict, tension, and explosive expression; sometimes with thoughtful analysis, understanding, empathy, introspection, and revelation. In short, to classify interviews and place them on the continuum of control provides a rough guide for analysis and discussion.

Interview Management: Control and Flexibility

The researcher needs to be alert to the ways control is used and for what purposes. Kahn and Cannell see the interview as communication; they define the information-gathering interview as "an interaction between the interviewer and respondent which both participants share," and note that "as in most communications processes, we have . . . two people, *each trying to influence the other and each actively accepting or rejecting influence attempts.*[1] [emphasis added] The connotation of "influence" is gentler than that of "control"; the latter term more clearly suggests the kinds of subtle or overt interviewer guidance seen in the following definitions and examples.

Maintaining control—a firm sense of direction—also includes a degree of flexibility, the capacity to depart from a set plan in response to unexpected turns or new opportunities. We will examine and compare the conduct of interviews with respect to both control and flexibility, considering the latter as part of an interviewer's control strategy.

In survey research or polling, the interviewer must be inflexible, bound to the predetermined wording schedule and sequence of questions. Even "branching"—providing for alternative directions—is pre-set and based on relatively few alternative anticipated answers. Truly open-ended questions require a different overall plan. To protect a survey's validity, neither the interviewer nor the narrator can manipulate the question schedule.

In contrast, the journalistic interview is usually controlled by the interviewer and permits flexibility. The interviewer may pose and restate questions, or try oblique approaches and other strategies to elicit a desired response.[2] The narrator of course can also be flexible, depending on knowledge, ability and willingness to respond, degree of candor, personal agenda, and the like.

Journalist Mary Ellen Leary observed that often the journalistic narrator has one objective in telling a story, whereas the interviewer has another. When Jerry Brown was governor of California he told her of an occasion when the *Los Angeles Times* sent a reporter to travel with him and conduct an interview.

> Brown said he deliberately tipped the reporter to a new policy he intended to inaugurate. I guess he wanted it to fly in the *Times* and see the response. [Brown] . . . was vastly annoyed and disappointed that this genuine tip never appeared in the paper. "He didn't even recognize that I'd given him a story," Brown said to me. "He was too absorbed in the line of questioning he had in his own mind to perceive something new."
>
> That struck me as a lesson. It illustrates how sharply different—even at cross purposes—are reporters and politicians at times.[3]

Perhaps in fact the reporter did not miss the point, but kept control of the interview, preferring to follow his own line of questioning, and resisting the governor's nudge to launch a trial balloon.

In both scholarly research and oral history interviews, narrators who control can also be flexible. Thus the oral history narrator often adds or rejects interview topics; the interviewer can ask, but the narrator chooses whether and how to answer. In addition, surprise sometimes supplements both flexibility and control. The interviewer's questions may prompt memory and free associations so that the narrator can spin a story or produce a spontaneous account, astonishing and delighting narrator and interviewer alike.

INTERVIEW TYPES AND CHARACTERISTICS

Focus on Examples

The following examples show shifts in the exercise of control, and the ways interviewers and narrators try to influence interview direction. We observe the survey research interviewer's instructions to adhere strictly to the question schedule, and see the journalistic interview's scope for contest of control. We can see how scholarly interviewers' checking back with sources cedes considerable control to the narrator, but also offers protection from error. In the oral history interview, there is virtually no contest. The narrator is usually unmistakably in charge. Finally, we see sub-categories of interviews such as dialogues and self-portraits being treated seriously enough to be subject to pointed and sometimes cantankerous criticism.

Survey Research And Polling

As we have noted, survey research and polling require the strongest interviewer control. Unless there is a way to record spontaneous comments that do not otherwise have a place in the schedule, the interviewer solicits and reports only those answers that fit. Thus the possible wit and wisdom of the off-schedule comments usually disappear. The survey or poll collects summary information involving population samples, rather than highlighting idiosyncrasies, individual differences, or the details of open-ended responses.

Survey manuals specify procedures. A survey (1) collects data "by interviewing a sample of people selected to represent accurately the population under study"; (2) asks each person "the same series of questions"; (3) organizes responses so that conclusions and generalizations can be drawn; and (4) uses precise interviewing procedures that are intended to "ensure full and accurate data collection."[4] The interviewer, who controls the proceedings and asks the prescribed questions as the manual specifies, is instructed to avoid signals of approval or disapproval that might introduce bias into the response.

The prescribed questions, or the individuals who create the question schedule, thus dominate control of the inquiry. The validity of the outcome rests in large part on the purpose and integrity of the questions. These can cover the widest range from a straightforward and neutral inquiry to one that is weighted, or even manipulative.

The public opinion poll, a sub-category of survey research, is probably the best-known type of survey.[5] The dictionary defines polling as "a canvassing of a selected sample group of persons to analyze public opinion on a particular question."[6] These neutral words describe a process that can create dramatic effects. The polls' prophetic power can magnify the significance of individual respondents' views so as to influence political processes, particularly elections. Such innocuous-sounding canvasses, condemned by some as self-fulfilling prophecies and hailed by others as authentic expression of popular views, testify to the expanding role of polling in forming, testing, and reporting public opinion. While the interviewer and the survey manual control the interview session, the product can launch significant consequences, to be discussed later.

Much survey research is conducted by university centers and private survey organizations, and many news organizations are now conducting their own polls. Governmental surveys such as the US Census are also significant.[7]

In England, a national census division sees its mission as a sort of communication outreach, emphasizing potential benefits to respondents. The Social Survey Division in the Office of Population Censuses and Surveys conducts sample surveys intended to act as a "bridge between the Government and the population, making it possible for the Government to keep in touch with the circumstances and opinions of the general public."[3]

In so doing, the division uses familiar definitions and instructions. It reminds interviewers that they are "with the informant in a business situation to collect data and not to tell him much about yourself." Otherwise, the interviewer might influence the informant, or vice-versa. Indeed, the interviewer might be "led away from the specific line of questioning, or, one could say, you (the interviewer) would have lost 'control' of the interview."[9]

Journalistic Interviews

The journalistic interviewer usually controls the conduct of the interview, typically controls the write-up, and passes it along to the editor. This is true whether the narrator is antagonistic, resistant, compliant, or cooperative. The effects of deadline pressures are often evident, and the interview style is sometimes, but not always, confrontational.[10] Some interviewers may guide, lead, push, or try to force the reluctant narrators into admissions and revelations. Others may obtain stories by negotiating, establishing rapport, and winning trust. The narrator's single most potent weapon is to deny access to the interviewer, although refusal may bring penalties. Other options include evasion, introducing other topics, or answering questions selectively.

When an interview-seeking journalist presses a request, a government official may react in various ways, sometimes punishing the individual by closing off access and thus controlling the flow of information. Under these circumstances, interviewers seem to accept their role as challengers, and journalists prize the probing investigative interview as the astronomer regards the newest star-probe. *The Washington Monthly* proclaimed:

> Our reporters go after information in the old way—they dig it up.
> They pester people. They keep on asking questions until they get
> what they need. They're not afraid to attack the pompous and
> the powerful to get to the bottom of a story. And their per-
> sistence has paid off big.[11]

Whether pompous, powerful, or down-to-earth, the public official-narrator pondering how and whether to talk to the press may find the access question already decided higher up. A newspaper account, "New Limits on Press Access Ordered by White House," stated: "The Reagan administration, in another attempt to control the release of information, has issued a sweeping order instructing government officials to clear all major press interviews with the White House." The order was reported to apply to "requests for interviews from print journalists as well as to requests for radio and television appearances." Further, it covered all subject matter and applied to a broader range of government officials than an earlier presidential directive that focused on "government employees' contacts with reporters on national security issues."[12]

"Clearance" by a governmental office is the key to control by limiting interviewers' access, whether at national, state, or local level. In a "whistle-blowing" incident like many others in government and industry, Dr. Donald Lyman, deputy director of the California State Department of Health Services, announced the "abrupt" removal of Chambers Bryson as chief of the food and drug branch and reassignment to "write a report analyzing the department and suggesting improvements." The story noted that "Other sources within the department . . . suggested Bryson's transfer was a result of his being too frank with reporters about department problems," e.g., that the "hiring freeze has caused inspections of food and drug manufacturers to be less thorough," and that food testing laboratories were being overwhelmed. In addition, "Lyman confirmed *it is a new department policy to clear all press calls through an administration spokesman.*"[13] [emphasis added]

Once the journalistic interviewer has succeeded in getting the narrator to talk, controlling the proceedings can be harder than it sounds, especially when the narrator's experience and sophistication outstrip that of the questioner. When Lacey Fosburgh granted an interview to one of her University of California journalism students, as the narrator she saw that the process was not working well for the interviewer. Afterwards, she wrote him a thoughtful memo of analysis, explaining why he must learn to establish and keep control: any narrator might do as she did, remain aloof and thus dominate the interview. Her comment underscored the narrator's ability at times to seize control by manipulative responses or by simply withholding answers.[14]

Further, an adept narrator who is determined to control can use prestige, apparent compliance, fancy footwork, or general deviousness, as Edwin R. Bayley reported in *Joe McCarthy and the Press.* Bayley quoted George Reedy who had covered McCarthy for United Press: "We had to take what McCarthy said at face value" because he was a United States Senator. The press is usually expected to be less credulous, but Reedy at the time apparently accepted this notion. Reedy noted

> Joe couldn't find a Communist in Red Square—he didn't know
> Karl Marx from Groucho. . . . Talking to Joe was like putting
> your hands in a bowl of mush. It was a shattering experience,
> and I couldn't stand it. Covering him was a big factor in my
> decision to quit newspaper work.[15]

In addition, Dan Hanley told Bayley about McCarthy's apparent cooperation when he checked back on a quote.

> I'd call Joe up and say this was the *Milwaukee Journal.* "Is this
> what you said?" "Sure," Joe would say, "I'll say that for you or

      do you want something else? How about this?" And he'd say
      something new. . . . "Tell me what you want and I'll say it."[16]
Here we recognize concerns about two kinds of verification. In the first, Hanley checked back with narrator McCarthy to see if the quote was correct. The second, an "obligation to verify" (in Mary Ellen Leary's phrase), related to the veracity of what McCarthy said. Bayley revealed the frustration of interviewers and other journalists, who knew that McCarthy was lying, but found it impossible to pin him down.

      [I]t was not enough to say . . . simply that McCarthy was lying, it
      was necessary to demonstrate the lie, and for a long time, as
      McCarthy shifted from one accusation to another, it was not pos-
      sible to prove that he was lying.[17]

It must have been painful for the interviewer who failed to verify because the issue also involved journalistic ethics (discussed in Chapter III).

    More typically, however, the journalistic interviewer can retain control through the write-up. South African journalist Anna Starcke's account of a taped session with Roelof Frederik "Pik" Botha is an example. She wrote,

      Partly because he had to get a lot of the things he had intended to
      say in New York off his chest—no matter what I actually
      asked—the one hour he had promised me stretched into three and
      a half. But since he got the chance to say them publicly three
      weeks later both in the US and locally, I have excluded most of
      that part of our conversation here.[18]

    Starcke combined three major steps in retaining effective control of the interview. First, she decided to control the content; second, she recognized that the narrator had taken over major portions of it; and third, she reasserted her control in writing up the story, excising the parts where the respondent had dominated. Whether or not the reader approves of her strategy, she was explicit and candid in explaining both the circumstances and the reason for her final deletions.

Scholarly Research Interviews

    The term "scholarly research," in "scholarly research interview," signals the primary interests and style of the interviewer (and sometimes of the narrator), and the kinds of uses the interview material is likely to enjoy. In addition to scholars, journalists and other interviewers at times conduct scholarly, if not research-oriented, interviews. The interviewers are usually professors, students, researchers, and other academics who seek information, illumination, and understanding. Informed narrators respond with facts, opinion, and interpretation. "Scholarly" and "research" suggest a high degree of care and accuracy, and frequently a willingness to check back with narrators to assure both accuracy of the accounts and continued access to that knowledgeable person.

    Gathering information for his book *Governing California's Coast,* Stanley Scott set up a program of scholarly research interviews. The interviews revealed what was happening in the early days of coastal governance by obtaining facts, interpretations, and opinions from the principal participants and observers. Here the scholarly research interviews, checked and rechecked with the narrators, supported a publication intended for use both by experts and nonexperts.[19]

The term and category—scholarly research interview—were coined for this analysis; they can be recognized both by what they are not and by what they are. Scholarly research interviews are not polling or survey research, but instead emphasize the individual, the personal, the unique. They are not journalistic: time pressure, if present at all, is relatively minimal, and the narrator has considerable control. Scholarly research interviews may be probing, but are not typically confrontational. They are not oral histories because the interviewer focuses on queries related to the research topic or cluster of topics rather than the recollections and life of a narrator. Again unlike oral histories, they are typically designed to serve researcher or research team, rather than the future use of many researchers, and the interviews are not designed for deposit in a research library or archive for subsequent use.

The scholarly research interview practiced at the Institute of Governmental Studies demonstrates a basic use—a session designed specifically to support a research project. A well-briefed interviewer, or more than one, conducts sessions with individual narrators. Control is shared. Individual sessions may last an hour or more, occasionally covering both scheduled and open-ended queries to elicit facts and views on governmental issues.

The interviewers and researchers write up the interviews; they place excerpts and quotes in a draft research paper and submit it to the narrators. The latter are encouraged to correct and/or amplify their remarks. The interviewer (or employer) controls publication.[20] (Checking back with narrators was an important element of this project, but is not necessarily characteristic of all scholarly research interviews.)

Narrators are usually chosen on the basis of knowledge of the field, up-to-date experience, and reputation for accuracy. Once the interview is underway, and also during review, the narrator can influence additions or deletions of quoted material. Thus the narrator's review can check for factual accuracy and interpretation, and can also determine the need for possible follow-up interviews.

The scholarly research interview can also take on the aspect of a dialogue between interviewer and narrator, and between interviewer (writer) and the community, when important public questions are at issue. For *Habits of the Heart,* the book's five-author team led by Robert N. Bellah approached "social science as public philosophy," seeking to "engage the public in dialogue." They also sought to involve specialists and experts through the primary device of research interviews they characterized as "active" and "Socratic." A thoughtful discussion of their preparation, approach, and technique stated the reasons why they did not use survey questionnaires or polling data: these provided "no dialogue between interviewer and interviewee," an important part of the process they sought to encourage.

Instead, they chose "active interviews" with a selective sample of citizens, to

> create the possibility of *public* conversation and argument. When data from such interviews are well presented, they stimulate the reader to enter the conversation, to argue with what is being said. Curiously, such interviews stimulate something that could be called public opinion, opinion tested in the arena of open discussion. "Public opinion polling" does not and might better be called "private opinion polling."[21] [emphasis in the original]

An intrinsic part of the book, the interviews dealt with individualism and commitment in American life through the views and often the actual words of the narrators. The interviews were designed and conducted to stimulate thought, argument, and public discussion, a valuable and distinctive approach in scholarly research.

Oral History Interviews

The practice of oral history as an art, craft, and research technique has many variations; definitions and examples used in this paper will not apply equally to all programs or projects. The discussion of oral history is based on the work of the Regional Oral History Office (ROHO) of The Bancroft Library, University of California, Berkeley.

Willa K. Baum, division head of ROHO, defined oral history: "Oral history is the tape-recording of reminiscences about which the narrator can speak from first-hand knowledge. Through pre-planned interviews, the information is captured in question and answer form by oral history interviewers. . . ."[22] She cautioned that "Oral history is not the tape-recording of speeches or other community events," and that "Oral history interviews differ from journalistic or specific historical research interviews in that they are intended for use in the future by a wide variety of researchers."[23]

At The Bancroft Library, oral history memoirs are "recorded and transcribed series of interviews designed to preserve the recollections and knowledge of a person who has played a significant role in or observed important events."[24] The terms "played a significant role" or "observed important events" include leaders, but also include participant observers who may witness and act, but not necessarily lead.

The inclusion of nonleaders is important. One critic of focusing attention exclusively on leaders, James W. Wilkie, coined the term "elitelore," which he characterized as based on the assumption that only leaders have memories worth recording.[25] In fact, classical oral history procedures work well with nonleaders, including members of ethnic groups who present community memories and knowledge of value and significance, such as Blacks in publications like *Drylongso*.[26] They may have participated in a group experience (e.g., Chinese immigrants detained on Angel Island, in *Island*[27]) or have experienced old age (e.g., aging in England, in *The View in Winter*[28])

These last-mentioned published works probably should be called semi-oral histories, since they omit the formal question-and-answer format that many in the field consider central to oral history. Ronald Grele, for example, described the oral history interview with its two identified participants as "a conversational narrative: conversational because of the relationship of interviewer and interviewee, and narrative because of the form of exposition—the telling of a tale."[29]

The writer, however, believes that the notion of "conversation" is of dubious use for oral history interviewers. A conversation can allow undue expression of the interviewer's opinion, gratifying but inappropriate, as well as questions half a page long that lead to narrator's answers of only a few words. "Conversation" suggests equality; "interview" suggests that the narrator does most of the talking and is expected to do so.

The oral history interviewer's style typically involves leaving the spotlight to the narrator (see also Chapter IV on technique). The interviewer nevertheless comes to the sessions with considerable information about both the memoirist and the material likely to be discussed. Such information does inform the questions posed and could be seen in other interview styles as opening a path to control. But in oral history the narrator has recourse, and can be led only as far as he or she is willing. However knowledgeable and subtle the questions may be, the narrator needs only say, "Let's not talk about that," and introduce another topic. Finally, if a narrator should be beguiled by the interviewer, a later reading of the transcript will quickly reveal any unwitting statements, and they will vanish with a flick of the narrator's blue pencil.

The transformation of a series of oral history interviews into a publication may blur definitions and usage. An example is Studs Terkel's rewarding book, *Hard Times: An Oral History of the Great Depression.*[30] While the book includes excerpts from a number of different interviews, and Terkel uses italics to identify the paragraphs he has written, he gives the reader no clue as to how the questions were asked, or what was cut from any narrator's response. Terkel does not say whether the narrators exercised any control over the interviews, or had an opportunity to review the material. He is silent on whether the interview transcripts will be placed in a repository for the future use of researchers. Such deposit is a prime qualification for oral history interviews, and is done whether or not the material is used for publication.

Control by the narrator (or interviewee) is a distinguishing characteristic of the classic oral history interview. Willa K. Baum has noted that such interviews are "checked and approved by the interviewee" before they are final-typed, indexed, bound, and deposited in libraries or other repositories. As suggested earlier, the narrator's review and approval of the transcript includes the right to change words, phrases, or as much of the narrative as he or she wishes to add or cut.

Admittedly, there are hazards in such control. A narrator acting as editor can suffer attacks of self-consciousness that a skilled interviewer can help to circumvent during interviews. When reading transcribed pages later, a narrator may become concerned that future researchers, posterity, friends, family, or critics may read the material and find it too casual, off-hand, colloquial, or frank. Such qualms and second thoughts may override the fact that the oral history interview is intended to recall memories. The narrator may try to "sanitize" it or transform it into a testament—proper, pompous, and dull. Fortunately most narrators make few changes, if any.

Most are willing to be revealed, warts and all, secure in the real control they exert after the material has been deposited, e.g., with a library or historical society, and made available for the use of researchers. Thus, by contract or agreement, the narrator can retain literary (publication) rights for a specified period or until death; can exert lifetime control over the use and length of direct quotations; or can seal part or all of the memoir so that it cannot be consulted until a specified date, e.g., a year after death, or a date chosen to assure that most or all persons discussed will no longer be alive.

Thus, the second vital characteristic of the oral history is the deposit of the full transcript and/or tapes in a repository that can discharge legal responsibilities. The library or historical society will safeguard the physical integrity of the material, and make it available as a raw primary resource for researchers, both present and future.

One can contrast the range of a narrator's control with that of an interviewer or another writer who knows that editors and publishers influence what is written, as well as whether and how the work is made public. The oral history narrator in fact has more control than a typical writer. No one is authorized to alter the text of interview material or influence availability or access. It is also understood, of course, that the narrator is providing primary research material, not an edited manuscript or finished work intended for publication. In short, it is appropriate for interview language to be easy, spontaneous, and colloquial. Free association is valuable and before responding to a question one need never hesitate to say, "I'm just guessing," or "I don't remember."

Some Eclectic Types: Dialogues and Self-Portraits

All interview types are not alike, and further, do not necessarily fit into the four categories identified here—survey research and polling, journalistic, scholarly, and oral history. While conversations and dialogues, biographical profiles, autobiographical self-portraits, or impressionistic man-in-the-street commentaries may resemble one or more of the four categories, they have their own important variations. A closer look at a few of these similarities and variations is in order.

One notable example is the "collective dialogue," as practiced by Irving Louis Horowitz. In the preface of his book, *Constructing Policy: Dialogues with Social Scientists in the National Political Arena*, he explained when and where the interviews occurred, and something of his own background. He noted that the interviews and discussions originated in an exchange program with professors from Princeton and Rutgers universities. Horowitz said he was able to "call upon scholars and researchers who . . . have had a long history of performing cross-over services between the academy and the polity." The focus was on a "collective effort to understand the content and context of policy making at national levels." He added that "the transcription of many reels of tape, repeated typescripts, and followup interviews . . . [made] sure that the final version fully represented the views held by each participant." Horowitz described his intent:

> This volume registers not simply a series of interviews, but in an exact sense, a *collective dialogue* in which I have sought to make clear the foundations of contemporary policy making.[31] [emphasis added]

His questions were sometimes directive and probing. A two-paragraph question/argument for Sar A. Levitan ended this way: "Would you not agree that this programmatic gulf has been strengthened by the negative attitudes of the conservative political establishment?"[32]

More challenging was his citing the narrator's previous position. Horowitz had prepared by analyzing the narrator's earlier writings that apparently contradicted a more recent statement. Horowitz said, questioning:

> In *The Promise of Greatness* you argue that these transfer funds are only marginally effective in determining the character of the economy. Now you are saying that these programs profoundly affect the character of the economy.[33]

These selected bits of evidence show the way the interviewer sought an accurate account, with check-back safeguards, but with his own strong control as he debated and challenged as well as questioning. Moreover, the interviews provided material for his own purposes. He was not so much seeking information and interpretation as evoking a dialogue/debate in which his own statements often extended from half a page to more than a full page in length.

Horowitz's approach is really that of a debate-dialogue, and does not fit smoothly into any of the other interview categories discussed here. The impact of Horowitz's personality and views, his equality of stance vis-à-vis the narrator, and the argumentative nature of the questions eliminate oral history as a close parallel. The challenge, and air of "getting the most," are reminiscent of the journalistic interview, while the stated purpose and repeated check-back resemble a scholarly research interview. The individuality of treatment would exclude the category of social science survey or poll.

Another variant form involves strong and self-willed narrators who dominate their interviews and develop what writer and literary critic Wilfrid Sheed has called their own self-portraits as revealed in what was then the most recent book in the *Review* series: *Writers at Work: The Paris Review Interviews*, Vol. IV. These interviews demonstrated narrators' control somewhat akin to that in oral histories. While virtually every interview revealed some aspect of the narrator's personality (and often that of the interviewer as well) willy-nilly, Sheed disapproved of what he saw as a deliberate pattern of control and even manipulation of the interviews by the narrators.

Observing what he called the narrators' "self-creation and self-concealment," Sheed noted disapprovingly that because they had the chance to

> revise their words and to erase the banalities of spontaneity, they are free to invent not only themselves, but their way of presenting

themselves: Stammers are ironed out, contradictions reconciled, mumbles turned into roars.

With respect to the interviewers, who remained faceless, he said

it is worth noting how much this particular skill [interviewing] has refined itself since *The Paris Review* started. . . . It is not easy to play the straight man, with a touch of the DA, to a famous writer; your own cunning must very nearly match his. And . . . you . . . disappear altogether leaving his answers standing alone on stage. Otherwise there is no art, only chat.[34]

Sheed continued to worry the question of whether the *Paris Review* interviews were or were not art (a problem we need not face in this study), concluding that "Most writer interviews are not art at all, but a sort of cultural packaging." He conceded, nevertheless, that all the interviews in the *Paris Review* collection were "self-portraits of the artist of a kind scholars are lucky to piece together, much less satisfactorily, from diaries and letters."[35]

Thus his analysis suggested that those interviews have much in common with oral history interviews: the narrator dominated, controlled, and finally reviewed and approved, while the interviewer—however skilled and well prepared—faded away like the Cheshire cat. (On the other hand, as we know, oral history interviews commonly reproduce the questions as well as the answers as a clue to the narrator's stimulus.)

Despite Sheed's cranky tone and his way of criticizing narrator-controlled interviews for not being journalistic revelations, his perception that such interviews are self-portraits is nevertheless useful and fairly persuasive. But he is unduly harsh, ungenerous, and negative. Some of his cavils are dubious at best: spontaneity is not necessarily banal; all corrections and second thoughts are not merely cosmetic and self-serving. Stammers and mumbles are tedious to read and the level of elocution attained in the original interview is of limited interest to most readers of published interviews.

Whether or not one agrees with Sheed's critique, his treatment is welcome for two reasons. First, he presented a serious evaluation of interviews as interviews, and gave attention to their conduct and presentation. Second, he highlighted a major difficulty in such evaluations: the ambiguity of expectations. He seemed not quite sure whether to judge the interviews as journalistic reports (presumably controlled by the interviewer), or as narrator-controlled efforts at literature. Despite these confusions in criteria, he recognized the value of the interviews as "the finest in literary shoptalk and exegesis," and added, "if that is not precisely literature, it will do."[36]

One can conclude that the *Paris Review Interviews* are titled simply and accurately. They make no claim to be other than they are, and still remain interesting and valuable enough to draw serious, if occasionally muddled, critical attention.

SUMMARY

Several things happen when two people talk in an interview. On one level, questions and answers move in sequence. On another level, control and flexibility (being able and willing to respond to another's wishes or adapt to new questions or topics) create the dynamics of the interview. Further, a political relationship develops as the interviewer and narrator sort out who will get what from the session.

The exercise or sharing of control differs with the interview style, and the process alerts the participants to the identity of the session: survey research and polling, journalistic, scholarly research, or oral history. We have seen how the interviewer exercises strongest control in survey research and polling, and next strongest in the journalistic interview. The narrator begins to dominate in the scholarly interview, and is in substantial control of the oral history interview.

Dealing with the principle of control and knowing who wields it is a useful first step in choosing and thinking about interviews and in understanding how one type differs from another. To the extent that other more eclectic types of interviews resemble the four selected here, similar notions of control can also hold true.

In addition, the interview ethics (how things should be done) and technique (procedures for getting them done) differ with each interview type. Thus depending on the kind of interview in question, certain kinds of behavior are ethically appropriate and certain kinds of techniques are suitable. Control is the simplest and most straightforward criterion in our analysis. With ethics, we move into a more philosophic realm and one more likely to involve some dispute; but even there we will find sufficient direction and agreement to point the way toward optimum interview performance.

III

Ethics: Trust and Responsibility

INTRODUCTION

Setting ethical standards for a single profession is a long, hard job, testing both practitioners and critics. To agree on standards for work engaging several professions as well as nonprofessionals and observers requires a mind-boggling effort, more likely to produce process than product. The differing styles, variety of practitioners, and complex of interests involved in interviews suggest both the difficulty of setting standards for their conduct and use and the need for such effort. It is something of a marvel that accepted standards do exist.

Professionals work with interviews as editors, interviewers, researchers, and writers, and sometimes narrators, in survey research and polling, journalism, oral history, and many scholarly pursuits. Amateurs also engage in these efforts, often seriously, and the readers or ultimate consumers cannot be numbered.

The search for acceptable standards takes two forms. The first relates to the fitness and propriety of behavior for the interview style in question. The second reaches beyond specifics to more comprehensive ethical principles, searching for common threads that can apply to the widest range of the interview experience. In her illuminating book, *Lying,* Sissela Bok suggested that

> Throughout society . . . all would benefit if the incentive structure
> associated with deceit were changed: if the gains from deception
> were lowered, and honesty made more worthwhile even in the
> short run.[1]

29

Bok tells us that candor does not win greater reward than guile as society works now. While no benefits are guaranteed for honesty, the examples and discussion that follow reveal the damage that dishonesty can cause. Consequently, honesty can appear more desirable, and perhaps attainable.

We begin with the assumption that honesty—as one aspect of ethical behavior—can be the best overall policy for each interview type, and consider what the full range of such behavior requires. We can watch for ethics in two aspects: the ethics of conduct and the ethics of use.

Ethics of Conduct

In conducting the interview, the interviewer usually has the advantage of speaking first, timing and "placing the pitch." That advantage does not necessarily last long, but it carries with it primary responsibility for identifying the type of interview, what is likely to happen to it, and other basic facts about the session. Methods of conveying information may differ, but the responsibility does not vary. Both the interviewer and the employer should be identified. This latter point is important because from time to time an unscrupulous interviewer has masqueraded as someone else—often a well-known journalist of good repute. When this happens, both the impersonated interviewer and the narrator are victimized.

Others also carry responsibilities. To be ethical, the narrator assumes an obligation to answer appropriately; the ethical editor—who links writer to user—assumes an obligation to avoid distortion in the published version. Further, the researcher who conducts his or her own interviews or uses those of others can either nullify the integrity of the original participants or protect it through accuracy in quotation, good sense in the choice of excerpts, and fairness in interpretation.

Ethics of Use

Issues of ethics in use appear most clearly in cases of *misuse:* the most grievous include varieties of distortion and the classic ethical lapse, plagiarism. To plagiarize is "to steal and use the ideas or writings of another as one's own,"[2] to gain value to which one is not entitled, while lessening the material's value to the original author. Plagiarism is unethical; the cure is attribution, accompanied by payment where appropriate. So much seems clear.

Not all unattributed use, however, is plagiarism, as when a journalist picks up what is in the public arena—such as a quote in a reliable newspaper to be used by other newspapers in subsequent stories. Such newspaper reuse is not considered plagiarism, while republication of another's material in a book is something else again.[3] Understanding accepted uses, and knowing what is and is not in the public arena are acceptable guides in these cases. Even so, when a journalist borrows "a quote" without mentioning the source, both the original narrator and the interviewer may well feel disgruntled.

Inappropriate use is another ethical lapse, more subtle but potentially misleading. If a researcher presents polling results as evidence of permanent and strong convictions on a public issue, such use is inappropriate and thus unethical. Consultation with reliable pollsters reveals that these captured opinions are momentary at best, and that the pollsters must be constantly on guard against potential distortion by the wording of questions or interviewer error.

Finally, to use a partial, edited quote is neither ethical nor unethical, per se. Caution is the watchword here. Excerpted quotes on book jackets and selections from movie reviews can raise more questions than they answer. Does " . . . riveting . . . " refer to the story line or to the sound track noise? Is " . . . revealing . . . " related to psychological insights, or a phrase that reads, "revealing an inability to act?"

NARRATOR'S ETHICS

Focus on Examples

The ethical narrator answers the interviewer's questions with as much candor as self-interest will permit. The examples show some narrators who are candid and some who are not. Some seem to puff the importance of their own actions while downgrading those of others, although it is hard to know how conscious the distortions may be. One deliberately tries to hoodwink his interviewer; another seeks to deny his own earlier statement, alleging that the interviewer was at fault. Still others are so concerned with accuracy that they check facts before speaking. Finally, an ethical narrator tries to uphold standards of accuracy by asking the interviewer to correct the latter's error, only to fail when the correction goes unreported.

Whatever their motives, these people captured by the snapshot of our examples reveal themselves by their actions. Their positions range from the embarrassing (unethical), through the equivocal, to the admirable (ethical). While ethics may not be their primary concern, we can evaluate the appropriateness of their behavior, taking into account what we think they owe the interviewer and the eventual user.

Narrator's Truth . . . The Whole Truth?

A narrator in a scholarly research interview may be asked for facts, impressions, and interpretations. In Scott's words, the interviewer seeks "the views and judgments of well-informed persons . . . who . . . have had relevant experience."[4] Narrators in scholarly interviews tend to respond to the best of their ability in part because of their own concern for accuracy. This attitude may be reinforced by an understanding that interviewers/writers will circulate one or more drafts for comment and review. Extensive revision and checking, of course, does not occur with all interviews: that effort requires time and patience, funding, and meticulous standards on the part of interviewer, researcher, and narrator.

Even with full review, interviews concerning the California coastal initiative reminded Scott that

participants' memories proved both retentive and inventive. (It is remarkable how many principal authors and architects can later be found for social inventions that begin to look successful.)[5]

In any event, the quality of the narrators' answers is crucial to the success of academic field research using structured or semistructured interview questions. Browning, Marshall, and Tabb gracefully noted this fact in their book *Protest Is Not Enough: The Struggle of Blacks and Hispanics for Equality in Urban Politics.* In two appendices they explained "Data," and "Indices and Measures," but stated in their acknowledgments,

All field researchers know that their fate depends on the forbearance of their respondents and we are no exception. The candor and generosity of our respondents, who generally suppressed their understandable hostility toward academics, were highlights of the project.[6]

Even when narrators are ethical and speak truthfully, they may not be fully informed. During and after the events of the Free Speech Movement on the Berkeley campus of the University of California in the 60s, the writer as a graduate student conducted a series of journalistic interviews with a variety of activist students. Questions concerned the drafting of specific demands and statements issued by Movement spokesmen.

At least three distinct groups could be identified in terms of meeting places and membership. Repeatedly, members of two or more groups claimed sole authorship of a particular statement. None said they knew of the others' existence or activities. Each expressed doubts that other groups could be reporting accurately, and yet each appeared convinced that its own claims were truthful.

In oral history interviews as well, the ability to recall, willingness to be candid, and the amount of time and energy available may support or impede the process of the interviews. Ethical performance does not imply "perfection," whatever that may be, but it does imply goodwill and the effort to implement that attitude. An insight into the narrator's ethical position is revealed, e.g., in an oral history brochure:

Because it is primary material, oral history is not intended to present the final, verified, and complete account of events. . . . it is the narrator's view, sometimes recounted in partisanship and passion, sometimes recollected in tranquility, always as perceived by someone deeply involved.[7]

Thus oral history becomes "vivid, immediate, and irreplaceable," as the narrator remembers and speaks. The freedom to speak or not, or even to remember or not, often appears to reinforce the narrator's own ethical scruples. Oral history transcripts show such narrator comments as, "I can't answer that. I don't know for sure."

In addition, some narrators' concerns for accuracy prompt them to document their own accounts. (Such preparation for oral history is neither required nor typical. The interviewer usually does the background research.) In the University History Oral History Series at The Bancroft Library, scholarly narrators include, for example, Katherine A. Towle, who consulted her extensive files and clippings about her career, including the years as dean of students at the University of California, Berkeley.[8] Further, Ewald T. Grether, dean emeritus of Berkeley's School of Business Administration, placed on his desk his own files that spanned more than 50 years of professional activity.[9] In the Knight-Brown portion of the oral history series on California administrations, journalist Mary Ellen Leary narrated her own memoir, and routinely consulted her collection of files, notes, publications, and clippings.

Musing on her experience as an interviewer, she noted the willingness of many people in academia and in government to be interviewed, and observed that they "recognize the important role an interviewer plays in conveying knowledge out to the user." She added that "On the whole, the value of imparting information (and hoping it's used honestly and advantageously) on the part of the narrator is a key part of the process. . . . I think our society, open as it is, encourages such a process."[10]

Oral history narrators may in good faith depend on fallible memories, sometimes with startling results. Interviewer Anne Hus Brower noted in the preface to interviews that focused on Walter Gordon:

> Walter Gordon has assumed larger-than-life proportions in the memories of his friends—in the literal sense; descriptions of him as a young man paint him as a giant, although his actual height was just six feet. As General William Dean put it, "Maybe I put more stature in him because of the man he was." This phenomenon accounts, perhaps, for his [Gordon's] being awarded three Big C's in the memory of one of his contemporaries when in fact he received only one.[11]

Narrator as Fact-Shader, Liar, or Faker

While ethical narrators try to tell the truth as they see it, those otherwise inclined may avoid the whole truth, or any part of it. Researchers may have to deal with an array of narrators who are flim-flam artists, deliberately devious, or shaders of the truth, as well as ordinary liars, full-time, part-time, or occasional. In short, the users of interviews must be alert to the possibility of falsehoods and half-truths.

In conducting or using interviews, one cannot always be sure which kind of narrator—candid or devious—is answering. An interviewer talking to the late Sinologist Sir Edmund Backhouse, "an impressive figure, with a long white beard, very much the man of letters," might well have found him both fascinating and convincing as he spoke of his literary friendships in Paris in the late 1880s.[12] M. Roland de Margerie, talking to Backhouse in Peking in 1943, was fascinated to hear Backhouse say that he had "even known Rimbaud at the time of his liaison with Verlaine, and [he] gave . . . details on that subject."

De Margerie was overjoyed with "Unpublished eyewitness testimony on Rimbaud and Verlaine, found in Peking! That was something to turn the head of any lover of poetry. . . . " The first draft of Backhouse's "The Dead Past," the second volume of his memoirs, had also mentioned Rimbaud, but a problem had arisen concerning the narrator's reminiscences. Professor Reinhard Hoeppli, the Swiss representative in Peking, had encouraged Backhouse to write his memoirs. When reading the draft, however, Hoeppli had "pointed out an insuperable chronological difficulty." Backhouse then "deftly changed the poet into a cobbler called Rimbot whose name had occasioned a temporary and pardonable confusion."[13] When historian Hugh Trevor-Roper sought to find the truth about Backhouse, he discovered "forgery and fantasy," identifying as fantasy the reports on Rimbaud. Trevor-Roper noted other long undiscovered duplicities that marked Backhouse's career, including cleverly constructed swindles and the invention of "historical" documents.

NARRATORS VS. INTERVIEWERS

It takes two people—the narrator and the interviewer—to build each interview; the ways these two compete, cooperate, manipulate, or understand each other shape the quality of the product. These relationships are crucial, and the understanding and practice of ethical behavior works toward the enhancement of understanding, if not cooperation. Alternatively, when ethical problems remain unresolved, the result is conflict.

Summary of Examples

Conflict can take many forms. One is denial of reports of what was actually said. In an odd twist, such denial may be offered not by a narrator objecting to the interviewer's report, but by a third party, one who was not present at the session. We observe that if the matter is significant at the White House level, the denial may be uttered by an unnamed "source." A more usual example shows conflict by simple contradiction: the narrator claims he did not say the words attributed to him, while the interviewer says he did, and offers evidence. Finally, narrator vs. interviewer conflicts, denials, and calls for correction can fuel a larger conflict, especially if it is enmeshed in an ongoing political struggle.[14]

Patterns of Conflict

Denials by unnamed sources. David S. Broder, chief political correspondent of the *Washington Post,* interviewed Secretary of Defense Melvin Laird

(June 27, 1973). Laird referred to difficulties in White House press briefings. Broder's story quoted Laird as saying that Nixon's press secretary, and later assistant, Ron Ziegler had a problem, and that Ziegler's deputy, Gerald L. Warren, should take over the press briefings.

President Nixon was staying at the western White House at San Clemente, where a denial was issued not by narrator Laird, but by "a source" who remained anonymous. The White House statement claimed: "The observation that Ziegler's usefulness is impaired is not shared by the President," and further that "Broder's story was not accurate on that point." Laird and Broder, however, had agreed that the entire interview could be tape recorded, and the tape supported Broder's accuracy. The lack of a narrator for the denial expanded the issue to include evaluation of an on-the-record statement vs. a faceless denial. *Washington Post* commentator Robert C. Maynard remarked,

> It is an important principle of political reporting that if a damaging assertion is made about an individual, no effort should be spared to reach that person and have his version of the story accompany the original contention.

But Maynard also pointed out,

> In this case, the original story was on the record and the denial was not for attribution. If such a denial is to be printed at all—and I am among those who question it—then the newspaper should feel obliged to explain to the reader that the original statement of Laird was tape recorded and the denial came from someone who would not associate his name with it.[15]

One can speculate that the somewhat oblique and anonymous denial was a device for disciplining narrator Laird, who presumably had no quarrel with the way he was quoted.

In the next example, the narrator challenged the accuracy of the quote, only to be confronted by a TV tape and transcript made by British Independent Television News (ITN).

Contradictions, or whom do you trust? In a brief story on July 21, 1973 the *Washington Post* quoted John D. Ehrlichman as saying that he was " 'delighted' to know the Nixon tapes had been made." The account continued, "Ehrlichman, interviewed by the British Independent Television News [ITN] said the tapes 'certainly should be produced for the committee.' "

The *New York Times* account of the event included this statement: "Asked if he thought the tapes should be released by the President, Mr. Ehrlichman said, 'Certainly.' " He spoke "only a day before the Nixon administration said that the tapes would not be released" to the investigating committee.

Ehrlichman contested the accuracy of the "certainly" quote. In response, ITN noted that the interview was on film. The tape and transcript presented interviewer Gerald Seymour saying about the tapes, "You'd want those produced, would you?" and narrator Ehrlichman responding, "Oh, certainly, certainly . . . " Seymour and ITN officials insisted that "not a scissors went in" to that part of the interview.[16]

The next example deals not with the eastern press, but with a California story.

Linkage of ethical issues. Decisions about interviews and their consequences pose questions of ethics and integrity that reach into the highest levels both in state government and in the press. Two sets of issues clustered around efforts in 1978 to prevent the confirmation of Rose Bird as Chief Justice of the Supreme Court of the State of California. The first group of concerns deals with interview ethics; the second, with related but broader issues of journalistic ethics.[17]

The day before the 1978 election, when the confirmation was subject to public vote, a *Los Angeles Times* story stated that the Supreme Court had "decided" a controversial case challenging a law based on *People v. Tanner* ("use a gun, go to jail").[18] The story alleged that Justice Mathew O. Tobriner, a supporter of Chief Justice Bird, had caused a delay in announcing the decision. To delay a "decided" case would be a serious matter. The assumption was that announcement of the court's unpopular vote on the eve of election would hurt her chances at the polls. The story further stated that Justice Tobriner had refused to comment on the allegation.

Interview ethics came to the fore in a subsequent news story again stating that Justice Tobriner had refused to comment. In fact, he had meanwhile told the interviewer that the allegation of delay was wrong, and denied that he had delayed announcement of a decided case. The interviewer was later unable to explain the errors in his second story and said further that he had erred in his first statement because he misunderstood the legal meaning of "decision" in a Supreme Court case.[19] Here the ethical issues involved failing to correct, and knowingly reiterating errors.

The second cluster of questions has to do with nagging concerns about journalistic ethics. Some unanswered questions include the ethics of the reporter's using a tip about Tobriner, the paper's decision to publish the story with only questionable verification, and the timing of such a story on election eve. These and other queries gave rise to speculation as to whether the paper was "used" for political purposes by those seeking to unseat Chief Justice Bird.[20] Finally, discussion about this episode reportedly included the statement that a newspaper "must publish" a story unless it can be proven untrue, a concept that turns on its head accepted standards of both ethics and decisionmaking.

INTERVIEWERS' AND EDITORS' ETHICS

The focus now shifts from the ethical problems of interviewer-narrator relationships to that of interviewer and editor. The narrators' interests are still present, but two other actors take over the action in the following examples.

Much of the responsibility for understanding and explaining interview conduct rests with the interviewer, whose job is to identify the interview type and be sure the narrator understands it. Thus a journalist should "show the notebook" or the tape-recorder that identifies the reporter; the oral history interviewer should explain the process of tape recording, transcribing, and approval by the narrator. Once the type of interview is understood, participants can recognize and accept procedures that are appropriate and reject those that are not.

Second, the interviewer should make only those promises that can and will be kept. The journalist can promise to submit the interview to a particular publication, but cannot say whether or when it will be printed. The oral history interviewer can state that the memoir will be deposited with a historical society or a research library, but cannot guarantee how many or even whether researchers will consult it. In addition, some additional burdens are accepted, e.g., by the journalist/interviewer who recognizes an "obligation to find out" not only for himself, but also for the public.

An ethical editor can question astutely, guiding the interviewer toward clarity on whether material is "not for attribution" so that the source is not to be identified. (If the interview is "off the record," the data cannot be used at all.) On the other hand, an inattentive editor can fail to spot errors in the written report, or in some instances, make them worse. (For discussion of the roles of editors and publishers, see Chapter V.)

Focus on Examples

Ethics-related tensions in the conduct of journalistic interviews tend to focus on the interviewer's efforts to preserve personal judgment and integrity, and also to deal fairly with narrators who may well feel injured if their names are sullied through erroneous quotes. Besides dealing with their own integrity and that of narrators, bona fide interviewers must also try to defend themselves against bogus interviewers, some ill-informed, others ill-intentioned.

We see examples of the ill-informed in the case of social science researchers cavorting like characters in *The Front Page* (Ben Hecht's satirical play on stop-the-press journalism in the 1920s). In this caper, the researchers appeared pleased with tricks thoughtful editors would no longer find acceptable. Equally at fault was a bureaucrat who fumbled badly as he tried his hand at interviewing.

We also observe the ill-intentioned who impersonated respected media journalists to gain access for their own purposes. Such chicanery completes the circle: the interviewer who misquotes or otherwise misuses a name does the narrator harm; and an interviewer who suffers impersonation or other misuse of his or her name receives a similar blow.

Promises, Promises

Codes of ethics provide some guidance, but the journalist/interviewer makes the decisions on the job. Personal judgment and ideas of fairness must fill in where codes are silent. Discussing the interviewer's approach, Lacey Fosburgh observed that people (narrators) like to talk and need to talk, but should also be made aware that they are talking to a reporter. Her solution calls on the journalist-interviewer to make sure the narrator "sees the notebook,"[21] or the tape recorder.

Edwin R. Bayley said that the journalistic interviewer should establish rules at the outset. Further, if a request for "off-the-record" treatment comes after an interview,[22] an interviewer should make no promise that an item will be withheld from publication.

Ben H. Bagdikian also raised warnings about a generally on-the-record interview in which, by agreement, one segment is to be kept off-the-record or non-attributable. In these circumstances, he urged that interviewers determine precisely when such an interview goes on-the-record again, adding still another caution regarding the need for clarity in defining what "off-the-record" means:

> The term off-the-record is widely misused. Even experienced officials and some journalists use it generically for any inhibition on disclosure. The interviewer should clarify whether the source means off-the-record (not to be used at all), or not-for-attribution (use it but do not cite me as the source), or background (use it as your own information). I have lost a few good stories because US senators misused "off-the-record."[23]

Bayley opposed making promises to narrators that they could review journalistic interviews. He believed the interviewer must take responsibility for accuracy, jotting down key words from a verbatim comment, and relying on his or her own notes and understanding. Much of a statement can usually be paraphrased accurately, with only a few telling words or phrases quoted directly. In general Bayley advised interviewers to avoid commitments and promises.[24] (For a slightly different view on checking back with the narrator, see Carol Lacey, below).

Concerning the use of direct quotes, journalist and editor Ed Salzman wondered about the inarticulate narrator who wants to answer but cannot find the right words. Salzman said that if he as interviewer suggests language the narrator likes and uses, he does not show those words in quotation marks when he writes the story. Instead, he presents them as a paraphrase.[25]

Uncertainty, and Avoiding Wrong Appearances

The foregoing examples emphasize clarity and precision in defining and setting conditions, and knowing when to check back, as well as when and how to use quotes. Good reportorial journalism at best, however, must deal with much ambiguity, despite the development of guides and codes. James C. Thomson, Jr., former curator of the Nieman Foundation, considered this ambiguity intrinsic to the profession. He noted that a journalist

> is unsure of his job's professional definition, unsure of the nature of "news," unsure of his organization's priorities, and unsure of his unique but fragile Constitutional protection. So along with the craft's great freedom comes multiple ambiguity and a vast amount

of ethical uncertainty. And that uncertainty is, in my view, both ineradicable and indispensable.[26]

Interviewers' commitments and decisions are usually upfront and visible. Less visible are the influences like gifts and favors that might obligate an interviewer to write a story that is more favorable than would be appropriate. Increased sophistication and sensitivity to even the appearance of improper influence has caused journalist interviewers and their employers to avoid accepting such freebies as travel costs. Mary Ellen Leary noted,

> There are occasions when payment for transportation may seem acceptable—i.e., when the only chance to interview someone would be on his plane flight somewhere, in a private plane. But usually now on presidential trips, reporters pay for travel (their papers or TV stations . . . do) *more* than first class flight rates, covering extra costs incurred.[27] [emphasis in the original]

Using My Name, or Did I Say That?

Naming the narrator is a key concern in the ethics of interviews; it is also an indicator of interview style. Survey research and polling, for example guarantee anonymity,[28] and to publish names or clues to identities would be a serious breach of ethics. By agreement between narrator and interviewer, however, scholarly research interviews normally do give the narrators' names, although on occasion it is advisable to identify narrators by codes known only to the interviewers and researchers while respecting anonymity in publication. Such coded identification permits researchers to write up findings accurately, but still use the screen of generic references in publication.

With respect to both scholarly and journalistic interviews, publishing the narrator's identity may add interest and significance. On the other hand, use of unnamed or unidentified sources often gives journalists increased access and at the same time may pose ethical problems unless narrator and reader understand the procedure. Interviews for "profile" articles or "conversations with . . . " as well as oral histories, gain much of their power and value from the narrator's identity. Occasionally, the identity of a prominent journalist as interviewer can be important as well. Finally, there is a similarity between an interview quote and a signed or byline article that links an author's name with his or her writings. In one sense, the whole article becomes a quote, and the writer takes on some of the vulnerability of a narrator.

The "power" of one's name, and the importance of protecting it from misuse, is an enduring concept in various cultures, and one that still carries a measure of acceptance in our own. Theodora Kroeber's *Ishi in Two Worlds*[29] shows an ancient, and extreme way of protecting the power of a name. When Ishi, sole survivor of the Yana Indians, was introduced into contemporary California civilization, those who came to meet him asked his name. No straight answer was possible, because "A California Indian almost never speaks his own name, using it but rarely with those who already know it, and he would never tell it in reply to a direct question." Seeing that some answer was necessary, Alfred Kroeber said, "he shall be known as Ishi," which in the Yana language means "man."[30]

Later, at a reception when Kroeber introduced visitors, he "was particular to pronounce the visitor's name distinctly, Ishi repeating it with great exactness and a disarming smile." Theodora Kroeber suggested that "Ishi's pleasure in the repetition of people's names was surely in part amusement with their strange sounds, but there may well have been an added fillip in saying it aloud and as it were promiscuously."[31]

Our culture imposes no such constraint on speaking our names aloud, but some ancient feeling for their power remains. Our names cannot be separated from our idea of ourselves; they symbolize personal identity. We tend to feel injured or cheapened, angered, when inaccurate quotes or misleadng contexts are linked to us by name.

Author and editor Norman Cousins was chagrined when a reporter misused one of his answers in an interview. As Cousins recalled the incident, the reporter asked

> whether I thought President Jimmy Carter is incompetent. My reply was: "Certainly not." The news story . . . began by quoting me as declaring that Jimmy Carter is neither an amateur nor an incompetent.

In Cousins's words, "Only a pompous ass would . . . make such a gratuitous remark,"[32] and he rightly resented the linking of his name with it.

Misquote and Rejoinder

Some injured parties do nothing other than to wait for the soothing effects of time when stung by a misquote. Others try to fight back. Dean Acheson is a good example of one with the means and the will to retaliate. His memoirs mentioned a press conference on September 26, 1952 when he responded to presidential candidate Dwight Eisenhower's address made four days earlier. Acheson said that General Eisenhower's statement

> purports to be a quotation, and an accurate paraphrase of a speech I made before the National Press Club in Washington on January 12, 1950.
>
> As stated it tortures the facts. It says things I didn't say and omits a significant and relevant part of what I did say. The General could have discovered this by reading my speech.[33]

More specifically, he added,

> General Eisenhower's combination of paraphrase and quotation left out [a] . . . warning [about a defense perimeter in Asia] and thus enabled him to . . . discuss the Korean situation just as if no such utterance had occurred and as if his own Government rather than the aggressor bore the guilt for Korea's tragedy.[34]

In responding to misquotation, Acheson had three points in his favor. First, as a former Secretary of State he was prominent enough to command public attention; he could call a press conference that attracted the media.

Second, the Eisenhower statement was made in a recent speech, so that listeners were likely to remember it. Third, Acheson's own speech was available and could be cited to support his defense.

A similar misquote of a well-known figure occurred in reporting a press conference. The print medium erred in its report of the event, and then behaved ethically by correcting the error. Spokesmen admitted, however, that the correction might not repair the damage.

In an appearance on NBC's "Meet the Press," January 13, 1974, Senator Barry Goldwater said that Harry Truman "is probably the best President we have had in this century." The next day, January 14, the *Washington Post* in a page-one story reported Goldwater as having given the accolade to Richard M. Nixon rather than Truman. On the following day the *Post* corrected the story in a prominent box on page one.

In an evaluative article on the incident, "Senator Goldwater and a Serious Gaffe," journalist Robert C. Maynard noted that not all the *Washington Post's* client newspapers used the correction, and that *New York Times* columnist Tom Wicker had written a column based on the original misquote. Further, Maynard noted, such errors in stories live on; they are "filed in libraries under 'Nixon,' 'Goldwater,' 'Presidency,' and 'Watergate,' and sit there 'waiting like time bombs for the unwary researcher of the future,' as Elizabeth Peer so ably put in *Newsweek.*"[35]

Interviewers Impersonating Interviewers

Journalist interviewers also can be victimized by impersonators. Patricia Lynch, a producer at NBC News, recounted experiences with followers of Lyndon H. LaRouche who "had played 'dirty tricks' on [NBC] . . . and interfered with its newsgathering activities by . . . impersonating NBC reporters and producers."[36]

Lynch also noted an interview she had taped with Sara Fritz, formerly a White House correspondent for *US News & World Report.* At the time of the interview Fritz was covering Congress for the *Los Angeles Times.* She told Lynch that

> in 1981 a LaRouchian woman had impersonated her [Fritz] to obtain important interviews, which then appeared under that woman's byline in various LaRouche publications. *US News & World Report* sued and won an injunction against the offending publications.[37]

The Bureaucrat as Interviewer-Reporter

Reminiscing about his years as mayor of Berkeley, California, Wallace J. S. Johnson recounted how the chief estimator for the Bay Area Rapid Transit District (BART) engineers fell into error through an aggravated case of selective questioning. Building plans for the transit system were in the final stages when the Berkeley City Council found itself in serious disagreement with BART's board of directors. BART and city estimates differed on the additional cost of building underground train tracks within the city limits, as compared to costs of building elevated tracks.

While other East Bay cities had accepted the idea of elevated tracks, Berkeley was determined to avoid creating a "right and wrong side of the tracks," believing that elevated tracks would divide the city physically and add to noise pollution. Berkeley also expressed willingness to pay the additional cost that underground building would create. The BART board was reluctant to alter its plans for Berkeley, and the cost of underground building became a major issue. The city estimated the additional cost at $11 million, while BART placed the figure at $22 million.

Contesting BART's figures, Berkeley sought to analyze the components of the BART estimate. City representatives and BART directors met 20 times; in one session, the BART estimator reported the alleged high cost of Montreal's subway, citing it as evidence to support BART's high figure. Johnson quoted the estimator as saying that

> Although he had never personally visited Montreal. . . . these figures were taken from information provided by Mr. Jules Archamboult [sic], Chief Engineer of the Montreal Transit Commission, April 9, 1964.[38]

When Mayor Johnson, himself an engineer, visited Montreal later that month, he discussed subway construction costs with Montreal's public works director and the assistant chief engineer. Their experience indicated that Montreal's construction costs were only about $6 million per subway mile, rather than the $10 million per mile the BART spokesman had reported. Johnson added, however, that he had also met another man in Montreal, Jules Archambault, chief engineer of the Montreal Transit Commission:

> We discussed coordination of bus and train schedules. He mentioned a ten minute telephone call on April 9, 1964 from "an estimator" for the engineers of the San Francisco Bay Area Rapid Transit District. The estimator apparently didn't know that the Montreal Transit Commission was a bus company, and had nothing to do with the design or construction of the Montreal subway.[39]

In this example, we see the bureaucrat-estimator failing as an interviewer by producing grossly inaccurate information. He misidentified the narrator, and compounded the error by failing to ask the most cogent question: "What is your experience in building subways?"

Tricking the Bureaucrats: The Masquerade

The romantic figure of the buccaneering interviewer/reporter may be somewhat out of date. Mary Ellen Leary recalled that when she first became a reporter there was a political reporter in town

> who operated only on the basis that anything on a public official's desk was public information and he had the right of access. He'd

walk into city hall—or the capitol—and pick up anything on a desk and read it . . . . [This] led to some angry scenes but he kept insisting it was his right and no one took him to court. I think today this wouldn't be tolerated by an editor.[40]

Even today, however, some social science researchers may use controversial techniques they usually associate with journalists.

Recounting their own views of interviewing, Becker and Meyers advocated a kind of low-level bribery, noting that in Chicago payment of a small sum often helped get answers: "to pay the two dollars . . . often speeds the information-gathering process."[41]

They also used the term "information interviewing" for practices they found

> most applicable when specific information is held by a limited number of people, treated as hard-to-get, and *must be obtained. . .* . [T]he universe is restricted to the few people who hold the information.[42] [emphasis in the original]

They explained that a visitor, preferably unannounced, who finds a "respondent" lunching at his desk, can "'speedread' his desk." The researcher/reporter lets his eyes wander, and reads "the documents and memos . . . lying on the bureaucrat's desk while carrying on a conversation with him."[43] The startled host may be too flustered to remove or cover papers while the intruders divert his attention. Such practices, however, risk loss of the public's trust in the researchers' integrity and fairness as well as in the validity of their findings. The researchers seem to fancy themselves old-style muckraking journalists. They appear oddly out of touch with many present-day journalistic interviewers who are more likely to outwit reluctant narrators than to outdo them in chicanery.

The researchers acknowledged that "many readers will be troubled" by the ethics of these tactics, but added

> [W]e feel that different types of social research cannot be conducted using one standard of ethics. Those who advocate stringent social research ethics often tacitly imply that we should be ethical because, if we are not, we will prey on all of our 'harmless' subjects. In our study, the subjects, political hacks withholding public information were not so harmless. The rules by which social researchers play should be determined by the nature of the game they are forced to play.[44]

In short, they see themselves and other social science researchers as justified in adapting their ethical standards to the game they think they are forced to play. But the judgment of some researchers may well be faulty or prejudiced when deciding who is or is not "harmless," and therefore fair game for trickery.

THE RESEARCHER AS USER, AND OTHER USERS

Researchers conduct interviews, and also use those conducted by others. Reusing interview material may pose sticky ethical problems. The first concerns judgment on crediting the original source. When the journalist as researcher picks up an item or a quote in a reliable paper and uses it in a new story, the source may or may not be credited. In this way, Mary Ellen Leary explained, one person's original material can be reused in various stories. "This is customary—picking and choosing from many different news clips." Such news material is considered "in the public arena."

But re-publishing in a book is something else again. The custom, as I've found it, when something is to be picked up then for resale, it is usual to write the publisher for permission; the publisher usually writes to notify the author, and often has a clause requiring payment to the original author.[45]

For preparing a book or article, other researchers would follow the second method. There researcher ethics requires full citation of the sources—in the case of newspaper stories to include page number as well as date, title, and name of the paper. Researchers using other published sources of interviews give credit as a matter of ethical behavior, to avoid plagiarism, and to observe the letter and intent of the law of copyright.

Second Use, and Sale of the Unused

The second type of ethical problem relates to a subsequent use of material in ways that might breach the original understanding between interviewer and narrator, or an unintended use that changes the nature of the material itself. Lacey Fosburgh addressed the use of interview materials in publications other than the original. She noted that a famous person may well complain, e.g., if an interview originally granted to a reporter for the *New York Times* is resold, reworked, and appears in a shoddy publication. She said that a journalist must take the narrator's feelings into consideration, adding wryly, "This is not altruism; the person might sue."

Fosburgh acknowledged ambiguities: some celebrities may want to be consulted regarding second use, and refuse permission. She thinks, however, that reporters do not have to make promises. If the narrator has willingly spoken to the press, the words are in the open and can be used—yet the speaker's feelings still need to be considered.

Inquiries may also come to an interviewer from "third-rate places" asking to buy information, material not used in the original published story. Fosburgh's advice: "Avoid them."[46] Caveats about this sort of second use are related to use of the interviewer's best judgment in winnowing material. Presumably the most reliable, significant, and telling details and quotes have already been selected and woven into the original story. If so, what is left unused may be of questionable value, the interviewer already having judged it too flimsy, uncertain, or unimportant to use.

Unintended Uses

Questions of ultimate use extend beyond journalistic writings and quotes to other areas such as oral history. Examples are ethical questions about (1) interviewers' obligations to warn of the likelihood of subsequent publicity; (2) possibility that the employer of an oral history interviewer may set inappropriate terms of inquiry; (3) concerns about the validity of oral histories produced by "commercial entrepreneurs" for other than historical purposes; and (4) distortion of an oral history when it is edited selectively for purposes of entertainment.

With respect to oral history interviews, a basic question must be answered: Under what circumstances can an interview or series conducted for one purpose and under one set of agreements be used ethically for another purpose? Oral histories edited for use as entertainment provide a case in point. Selected passages can be excerpted from the tape or transcript of one or more interviews and assembled for radio broadcast, with theme and pace determined by the show's producer.

As portions are edited to fit the focus and time available, subtleties, qualifications, and balance can be diluted or lost. The thought and judgment evident in many oral history interviews may be pruned away, and the raw incident, devoid of context and explanations, may be funny, dramatic, or exciting, but such presentation also can become distorted and "untrue." Editing for entertainment is different from editing or quoting in research papers, in part because the latter can include qualifications and disclaimers that the entertainer would find "dull," and unsuited for the entertainment format.

Here the name "oral history interview" is significant. Interviews conducted for entertainment purposes are "interviews" that meet those criteria, but are not "oral history interviews," which are primary research material. Oral history interviews are conducted for deposit in research collections for scholarly and thoughtful use. It is the user's understanding, not the medium, that signals propriety.

While the researcher who reads and uses oral history memoirs may be intrigued or amused by some of the contents, the principal purpose is to gain information, clues, and understanding, rather than to be entertained. The demands of entertainment—crispness of pace, tension, conflict, frequent laughs, manipulation for effect—can seriously distort the content and context of the narrator's oral history material. Further, editing for entertainment may trivialize the material, failing to do justice to major themes and oversimplifying by emphasizing only selected passages or excerpts.

To manipulate material for entertainment means pulling out the amusing, colorful, dramatic or sensational bits, with the risk of endangering the full content and meaning of an interview.

The TV interview is not officially part of this study, but is so pervasive and familiar that it should be noted as an example of the conflict between interviewing for information and the interview as entertainment. A number of TV interview programs are informative; they must also be entertaining, stimulating, and possibly exciting as well, or viewers will turn the dial or punch the remote control button. Thus TV interviews can and often do produce valid information, but those that consistently lack the entertainment component are not likely to hold their audiences.

SETTING STANDARDS:
UNDERSTANDINGS, CODES, GUIDELINES

We have seen efforts to deal with ethical issues and observed some pit-
falls for researchers who conduct or use interviews. It seems clear that participants and users, whether amateur or professional, need the firm base of ethical standards. As noted earlier, professionals bear the heaviest responsibility
for identifying and setting ground rules. The following pages review some
examples of guidelines and codes of ethics professionals have developed in
oral history, journalism, and survey research. To be sure, ethical rules and
statements of intent alone do not guarantee reliable performance, but they do
provide a necessary first step.

Focus on Examples

Guidelines and codes can help suggest ways to resolve ambiguities in
the obligations between individuals and theirs to society. Pragmatic guides
can address human problems and motives that shelter behind noble slogans
such as "the First Amendment," "research for Science," "the evidence of History," "Freedom of the Press." Splendid-sounding concepts alone are not
enough to help solve real problems; these require down-to-earth practice and
decisions.

The following examples include some highly developed and widely
accepted guidelines, e.g., those for oral history interviews. Such rules should
not be regarded as the final word; guidelines are typically in the process of
development. At their best, guidelines and codes offer ways to resolve
conflicts, protect legitimate interests, and support and strengthen professional
conduct. We can evaluate these codes by how appropriate, consistent, enforceable, and inclusive they are and the precision and clarity with which they pinpoint responsibility and spell out obligations.

Oral History Guidelines:
"Who Needs to Know What?"

Of the three disciplines—journalism, survey research, and oral
history—the last is the youngest. It developed in its present form shortly after
World War II, during an era increasingly concerned with professional ethics.
This timing may help explain why oral history interviewers have accepted a
coherent body of directives about ethics, conduct, and mutual responsibilities,
apparently with more ease than in other fields. Despite the existence of
comprehensive guidelines, however, changes and expansions of the field will
continue to require periodic review to keep them current and effective.

With the increasing popularity of oral history interviews the Oral History Association has developed guidelines for use in evaluating oral history
projects.[47] "Ethical/Legal Guidelines," for example, pinpoint the responsibili-

ties of both interviewers and interviewees (narrators). Guidelines require assurances that both parties are "made fully aware" of their rights and interests, of ethical and legal responsibilities to each other and to the program/project, of eventual placement of the interviews in a suitable repository, and of possible uses of the material, as well as procedures for release by the interviewer, and deed of gift or transfer from the narrator.

The guidelines further specify that oral history staff members must understand the need for confidentiality until the interview is released; and conduct interviews "in a spirit of mutual respect and with consideration for the interests of the interviewees." They must also demonstrate ability to carry out legal agreements and protect both tapes and transcripts from unethical use; and finally to gather accurate material, process it as quickly as possible, and make it widely available. Thus oral history practice focuses on communication between interviewer and narrator, explanations of the process, mutual understanding, scrupulous adherence to agreements, and full discharge of responsibilities.

Agreement has become increasingly important as oral history has expanded from its initial role of providing source materials for deposit in university or public archives and special collections. This role continues to be significant, but oral history has expanded to include many others Some newer developments include "Public history, where scholars are hired to help government agencies, private foundations, or other groups chart their pasts"; and "local community history . . . . non-elite, community based."[48] Oral history also provides significant elements in historic preservation projects, as well as material for the entertainment, or story-telling business. The range and variations of material and uses expand the opportunities for abuse, e.g., invasion of privacy, conflict of interest, commercializing, selective editing, and piracy.[49]

Codes of Ethics for Journalists

Establishing a professional code of ethics seems laudable, but it is nevertheless controversial, and prickly issues soon arise around ethical questions. Who should establish codes for journalists: the working press itself? publishers and editors? local press councils? a National News Council? Should organizations of journalists make the decisions, or individual practitioners consulting their own consciences? At least a score of journalism codes exists nationwide, but the debate continues on who should do what. A sampling of the discussion, explanations, and justifications may help clarify the key points of view and of conflict.

The News Council, founded in 1973 and dissolved in 1984, during its lifetime stated that it was:

an independent, non-profit, voluntary organization . . . representing varying occupations and shades of opinion. Assisted by advisers and a small skilled staff, it examines complaints received about inaccuracy and/or unfairness in news coverage, or unethical conduct by a news organization.[50]

The Council aimed "to uphold the principles of the First Amendment and to protect the nation's news organizations from unfair attack." The council also noted that it had *"no power to regulate or impose penalties."*[51] [emphasis added] It sought to promote "truth and fairness in news coverage," but did so without promulgating its own code. Thus the National News Council, unlike the council in Great Britain, had no authority to require adherence to any specific rules, nor perhaps more importantly, to require papers to print announcements of council rulings whether favorable or not.

The council's philosophy pinpointed its essential weakness. In answer to a direct question, Executive Director William B. Arthur explained that the council

> does not have guidelines, or a code, covering the matter of ethics in reporting, nor does it plan to issue such guidelines. . . . [The Council feels that] it is the responsibility of the press itself to issue, or not issue, as it sees fit, guidelines covering reporting efforts.[52]

He candidly added that "Much of what comes before The Council is concerned with the accuracy and fairness of quotations," but said that there is no way of knowing what may have been deleted when the complaint was made and the evidence produced.[53] He noted that

> There can be no arguing that the responsibility for publishing or broadcasting quotes accurately is shared by the reporter, the editor or news director, and by the news organization itself.[54]

Since ethics in reporting—much of it based on interviews—is so central to the practice of journalism, it seems strange that the council treated this important and sensitive area with averted eyes.

The idea of shared responsibility for codes is reflected in Bruce Swain's observation in *Reporters' Ethics* that the job of developing enforceable codes has been left to individual papers. Swain noted that sometimes management alone writes the codes, and sometimes reporters and management representatives work together. In fact, the National Labor Relations Board (NLRB) has held that "management had the right to impose an ethics code, but . . . its penalties must be bargained with the union."[55]

Swain further noted, however, that a double standard of conduct often prevails for reporters and for publishers and editors. He asked, "If codes are effective in bolstering reporters' ethics, should not publishers and editors adhere to the same rules?" He added that "At some papers, especially those notorious for the strong conflicts of interest of their owners, proclamation of codes of ethics for *reporters* strikes observers—especially reporters—as ironic."[56] [emphasis in original]

Debate continues on who has the "right" to establish a code of ethics. The National Labor Relations Board has expressed two divergent opinions about whether publishers can set codes unilaterally, or whether newspaper employees—members of the editorial staff—must be involved in negotiations. In the 1975 *Capital Times* case, the board held that when a publishing company provided a code of ethics it was also dealing with regulation of working conditions; consequently the code must be subject to bargaining with the employee's union. The next year, however, the NLRB reversed itself and declared that "newspapers have the right to adopt codes unilaterally."[57]

By whatever means they are established, 10 codes of ethics are available for comparison in the appendices to Swain's book.[58] They reveal the relative values assigned, e.g., to concepts such as gifts (freebies) and conflict of interest, impartiality, responsibility and fair play, as well as specifics such as accuracy and the correction of errors in news stories.[59]

Five of the 10 codes did not deal with ethical standards for interviews. (This tally counts those of the *Louisville Courier-Journal* and *Time* news/editorial/photo staff and management as two separate codes.) Even the five that dealt with the conduct of or reporting of interviews, or the integrity of quotes, did so primarily by implication or allusion, e.g. "Persons publicly accused should be given the earliest opportunity to respond." Statements referred to the use of anonymous quotes, confidentiality of sources, or the inclusion of "comment from persons accused or challenged in stories," but did not discuss the actual treatment of quotes.

Interestingly, where specific conflicts or financial problems were mentioned, they were spelled out in detail. Five of the ten also referred in a general way to responsibility, fair play, accuracy, and correction of error. Four specifically mentioned quotes, and one referred specifically to interviews.

Those who attempt to write ethical codes deserve sympathy, along with the criticism that inevitably seems to be their lot. Codes of professional ethics can conflict with other significant rules. In fact, Ben H. Bagdikian pointed out that "in some instances a code of ethics may conflict with the First Amendment." As an example he cited a ruling by the Securities and Exchange Commission whereby financial writers are required to print their personal financial interest in companies they write about in such a way that stock prices could be affected. He noted, however that "the First Amendment forbids mandatory printing of anything." Commenting on the ethical principal involved, he said, "Nevertheless, it is both unethical and illegal for a writer to benefit directly and knowingly from stock price changes produced by what he or she writes."[60] Here the conflicts of ethics and interests bring together at least three concerns. They include the interest of the public in avoiding manipulation by the press, the concern of the columnist or interviewer to write fully and freely without undue restriction, and that of the press as a professional group to defend its constitutional rights.

Summary

This brief overview finds journalistic codes offering little ethical guidance to the reporter as interviewer. A few precepts by colleagues may help the reporter-interviewer stay on track. These can be stated as cautions to: "place between quotation marks only what the narrator says," "Paraphrase for succinctness, clarity, and accuracy as needed; use quotes only for the most telling words or phrases," and finally, "If the narrator didn't say it, don't quote it."

Elsewhere in this discussion, experienced journalists have stated some of their own maxims for interviews, designed as much for self-protection as for that of narrators. The themes are to let narrators know that they may be quoted and to avoid making commitments regarding use of the material. Their rules-of-thumb can be paraphrased, e.g., as "Don't make promises you can't keep," and "Let them see your notebook" (or tape recorder) that identifies the journalist.

Survey Research, Informed Consent, and Quality Control

Protecting the subject's interests. In survey research and polling the interviewer is in control and bears major responsibility for ethical performance. (The interviewer may be termed the investigator or researcher; the narrator is also called the respondent or the subject.)

One survey research guide comments: "The data collection phase of the research process is one . . . where you are most likely to encounter questions of ethics. Report preparation and publication is the other."[61]

Because the interviewer is in control, and there is a potential for injury to a respondent, the literature of social science research discusses "informed consent" and the use of contracts between the researcher-interviewer and the subject-respondent. Such contracts are intended to protect the interests of human subjects (the respondents). Bower and de Gasparis noted a variety of protections dealing with privacy and anonymity, and such concepts as responsibility and commitment. Examples included specifying the form for storing the data, and providing "full identity of investigators, those who acquire the information, and . . . [their] relevant auspices. . . ." Another major point dealt with possible deception and conditions for disclosing it. Finally, discussion of the ways results are to be used embraced the "nature and form of any publication, including steps . . . to protect the integrity of private matters in any public use of information."[62]

In the paraphrase by Bower and de Gasparis, the American Psychological Association general code stated that "Research should begin with an agreement between investigator and subject concerning the responsibilities of each, and the investigator is obligated to honor all commitments."[63] The goal is to protect the subject of social research from such risks as coercion, deception, invasion of privacy, breach of confidentiality, and stress. In addition, the code seeks to prevent harm to others.

Informed consent can include setting specific terms of agreement and signing consent procedures. Such procedures are often followed in social science research and oral history interviews, but are notably absent in typical journalistic interviews. Signing and filing consent documents is acceptable in the first two, but for the journalistic interview, the more casual informed consent is usually shaped by the style, assumptions, and personal ethics of the interviewer.

Confidentiality and partnership. Confidentiality is a major element in the ethical ground rules of survey research, including occasions when participants answer self-administered questionnaires. Survey researcher Mervin D.

Field noted that survey researchers frequently combine questionnaires and telephone interviews.[64] The phone interview is used to identify qualified respondents, who then receive the self-administered questionnaire, sometimes accompanied by visual material. The interviewer's second phone call completes the sequence. Alternatively, the interview-questionnaire material can be mailed first, with the respondent calling the interview number when ready to participate in the spoken interview. Field also noted a requirement that if a survey researcher wants to return to continue a longitudinal study, the researcher must ask the respondent's permission to do so.

He explained that his organization guarantees confidentiality to respondents by removing all names and addresses from questionnaires. One purpose is to avoid a possible problem if survey research material were to be subpoenaed as evidence in a court case. To leave names and addresses still attached would be a clear breach of confidentiality, and counsel could call respondents to verify answers or to solicit further information. Field said that his organization has pioneered in gaining court acceptance of survey research evidence, with respondents unidentified.

He also referred to two organizations with appropriate codes of ethics: the American Association for Public Opinion Research and the Council of American Research Organizations. The former said flatly, "We shall protect the anonymity of every respondent." In addition, *A Guide to Professional Ethics in Political Science* by the American Political Science Association lists a variety of topics under "Scholarship." Among others, they include "The Scholar's Ethical Obligation to Protect Confidential Sources," Advisory Opinion No. 13 (August 16, 1973); and "Plagiarism," Advisory Opinion No. 16 (May 17, 1975).[65]

Field observed that survey researchers understand the partnership aspects of their work with the public and find the interaction a "precious resource," to be valued and protected.

Presenting and evaluating the product. To maintain a high level of quality in the survey product is an essential part of the interviewer's ethical responsibility. Such quality control includes subsample rechecks through reinterviews and post-enumeration surveys (PES). These efforts focus both on whether "interviewers are going to the right units and on the general quality of the interviewing . . . in order to estimate the amount of response error." In *Reasoning and Research,* Thelma F. Batten observed, social scientists understand that

> it is no disgrace in science to have to work with data that are not as adequate as you might like. Disgrace, if any, comes because you have not made your basic observations . . . as accurate as was practical, or—much worse—if you pretend in your report that your data are more accurate than you know them to be.[66]

CONCLUSION

We have looked at examples of ethical problems in interviewing and some solutions proposed in the form of codes and guidelines. The narrator (subject), the interviewer, the researcher, and the editor all have major roles. Since their interests often diverge, can they all be accommodated? Presumably they can, at least in part, by recognizing the specific types of interviews and clarifying the appropriate expectations of each participant.

While general good will is an important component in ethical behavior, practice demands specifics. Clearly, thought should precede action in interviewing, with patterns established before pressures begin to rise. Interviewers with pencil or telephone in hand, or fingers on the "record" button, do not pause to examine conscience or review ethical principles. Editors or narrators on the firing line of deadline or confrontation are not likely to weigh the finer points of ethical behavior. Nevertheless, even when an event is underway, it is not too late to make ethical judgments and decisions. Many practitioners do precisely that as a matter of course.

Well before the action starts, however, is the time to begin thinking about how to function. Even with careful advance planning, the unexpected can make judgment difficult. Bagdikian noted of the journalistic interview: "Often an interview, spontaneously and dramatically, takes a radical turn in direction and significance that cannot be predicted in the usual pre-interview understanding."[67]

Practical-minded professional groups seek to maintain standards by enacting codes of ethics. In general, they try to promote the trust and integrity that philosopher Sissela Bok calls "precious resources, easily squandered, hard to regain," and that require a firm foundation of "respect for veracity."[68] While these truths may seem virtually self-evident, and few will argue against such ethical principles, ethical practice can be another story, as several of the examples demonstrate.

Some individuals respond to pressure with haste, fatigue, misjudgment, carelessness, and role confusion. Others manage to keep their balance and their promises, while still getting the job done. They know how to combine skill, training, clarity of understanding, and hard work to perform ethically as they conduct an effective interview and use it correctly.

The professions' codes of ethics vary in what they emphasize. For example, oral history guidelines and those of survey research stress clarity of agreements and protection for the narrator or respondent. Both carry an implicit injunction for the interviewer: "Do no harm" to the respondent or to the truth.

Journalism codes admonish interviewers to refuse gifts and freebies, and to avoid conflicts of interest. A relative few also focus on such ethical aspects as ensuring fair play for the narrator by quoting accurately, and by providing suitable opportunities for reply and correction in case of error. The ethical stance and performance of the interviewer come first; dangers or benefits to the narrator are secondary. The signed consent documents that are suited to oral history and some social science research fit less well in the more free-wheeling journalistic interview. Variations occur because interviewing remains a craft, if not an art, a mutual human endeavor where ethical principles are often honored in theory, while practice may lag behind.

Interviewers can be admonished to follow professional codes, and to internalize ethics; respondents/narrators can be urged to answer as fully and honestly as their own self-interest permits; and editors can be counselled not to tamper arbitrarily with the material submitted for publication. Such mutually ethical behavior permits mutual benefit. Codes and guidelines help encourage and protect the patterns of behavior recognized as ethical, although they cannot guarantee it. Pragmatically, however, when ground rules for each type of interview are followed, the quality, reliability, and amount of useful information and insight produced should more than justify the time and effort they require. Further, such observances help participants fulfill ethical responsibilities to the public as ultimate users, as well as to themselves.

For participants in all types of interviews, a key ethical message can be stated this way: Know what you are doing and make sure others know. Say what you are going to do, and do it. Keep your word before, during, and after the interview.

Ethical principles provide insights into what can and should be done in each type of interview. How it can be done is a matter of technique and skill, to which the discussion now turns. Ethics and technique are examined separately, although it is clear that they are closely linked. In fact, understanding ethics furthers the productive use of the talents and energy needed for first-rate technical performance.

IV

Technique: Skills and Suitability

INTRODUCTION

Interviewers' techniques build interviews as fiber artists' techniques create works of art. The artist plaits, twists, compresses, weaves, knots, twines, or embellishes, choosing both materials and techniques to produce the object. Similarly, the skillful interviewer selects topics, narrators, and techniques to produce the style of interview desired.

Interviewers' techniques include finding the right narrator or narrators, gathering and preparing information, using suitable ways to pose questions, and finally presenting the outcome. In short, the interviewer needs to know the topic and the interview's purpose, understand when and how to ask the right questions, and know how to listen, as well as when or whether to interrupt and direct. The interviewer must know how to choose and use tools properly: the computer for survey research phone interviewing, the tape recorder for oral histories. Finally, technique includes shaping the material for use, and understanding whether time is an ally or enemy for the job at hand.

The discussion examines two pairs of interview styles. The first consists of journalistic, and survey research and polling interviews. They are often concerned with similar topics and time pressures, particularly when polling addresses political questions. They demonstrate the symbiotic relationships among media concerns, journalistic interviewing, polling, and interpretation of poll results.

The second interview pair, scholarly research and oral history interviews, also share some similar time perspectives. Although scholarly research interviews are often on the cutting edge of events and policy changes, they are usually less deadline-oriented than those in the journalistic or survey-polling style. Further, oral history interviews that capture and preserve primary source material for future research escape all deadline pressures save those imposed by narrators and interviewers, or by funding sources.

Along with the relative influence of time pressures, it will be useful to look at other concerns, e.g., the quality of the interviewer's preparation and the way the interviewer performs in action. We turn first to the journalist.

ASPECTS OF THE JOURNALIST'S APPROACH

A Journalist's Interviews

Journalists' interviews bear a distinctive stamp, whether written as breaking news stories, ample *New Yorker* profiles, or books that may take years to complete. An interviewer is more free and self-directed in journalism than in survey research and polling. The journalist often seeks out narrators who are unique and idiosyncratic rather than "representative." In contrast to an oral history interviewer's quiet encouragement and acceptance of the narrator's account, the journalist's approach can be challenging, even antagonistic.

In Lacey Fosburgh's view, the journalist does whatever is needed to get "the most" from the narrator, to "pick the lock" to reveal information that otherwise would remain hidden. The resulting interview serves a variety of purposes: it can be the full story or a source of background, interpretations, clues, and verification. Fosburgh sees the reporter and the editor working out an agreement on the story, while the reporter/interviewer provides special angles. The editor, nevertheless, makes the assignment and defines the story. The reporter can add to and change the story concept, but is answerable to the editor as part of a "rational professional system."[1] In short, the journalist's responsibility to the editor inevitably influences technical performance.

Focus on Examples

The following discussion and examples highlight features of journalistic interviews that distinguish them from other types. Importantly, the examples also allow us to see journalists using their techniques in action, fielding opportunities and difficulties as events and faces rush by.

At the crossroads of theory and practice, we see the journalist-interviewer finding the narrator and getting the story. Ideally, the interviewer is a well-trained specialist with ample time for preparation and reflection. In reality, often the interviewer is a general-assignment reporter with only "general" knowledge and no time to prepare for his interviews. Moreover the story is due "now." In the circumstances it is sometimes amazing that the interviewers get anything at all.

The examples show people operating under pressure: journalists using skills ranging from friendly rapport to open confrontation, with some narrators cooperating and others trying to manipulate the interviewers. Meanwhile, both parties tend to seek ingenious ways to protect themselves and their own interests.

The Journalist's Identities

Among the interview types under study, the journalistic interview is the most ambiguous with respect to guidelines and techniques. The interviewer is at once an entrepreneur, an adversary, member of a group of peers,[2] employee of a publisher and "natural enemy" of many editors, and a worker clothed in the majesty of the First Amendment.

With such complex identities, the journalistic interviewer requires, but often does not achieve, in-depth preparation. Equally important is the skill to probe for revealing answers.

On Being Overawed and Silenced

Control remains a significant element of journalistic interview technique, whether the interviewer is pugnacious or sympathetic. When Theodore E. White was an inexperienced young reporter interviewing Mao Tse-tung during the era of the Chinese revolution's "Long March," he deferred to the formidable figure and made no effort to probe or challenge. The two were in Mao's wartime cave dwelling, and White recalled his feeling that

> [Mao] must not be interrupted as he thought. And he was thinking aloud to me as he rambled. There was no dialogue; I was a student; he was instructing me. . . . I did not think then to ask him who would define what an enemy of the people was.[3]

White's experience was atypical, but clearly outlined the consequences of confusion. His candor revealed the way the young reporter lost his sense of role; from interviewer he slipped to student. It is less clear whether Mao would have permitted an interruption to his monologue, or whether he would have responded to the probing question that a mature White wishes he had asked. Even so, White implied that his real task was twofold: not only to keep Mao talking, but also skillfully to insert the telling questions that could push the narrator to think anew and to reveal his thoughts.

Preparation and the Searching Question

Inadequate preparation, or none at all, can mar performance at interviews and news conferences alike. When Diana Tillinghast reported on a study that included the *Erie Morning News,* she recalled that the paper's city desk had two days' warning that a political candidate was to be in town. Nevertheless only ten minutes before his arrival, the paper assigned a police reporter to cover and participate in the news conference. She noted,

The police reporter had time to grab *Time Magazine* and brief himself on what *Time* said about the candidate while he was driving to the press conference. His question . . . was something like "How do you like Erie?"[4]

The reporter predictably failed as an interviewer: he lacked preparation, story sense, and political awareness of the event he was covering. Luckily, this was a press conference with multiple participants. A one-to-one interview would have been a disaster.

Challenge or Rapport

Legal tradition, culture, and training give an American journalist a full repertoire of interview techniques and strategies, from gentle queries and sympathetic listening, to well-informed probes, to vigorous challenges or even confrontation, with tenacious follow-up. Compared to colleagues elsewhere, the Americans are sometimes seen as having higher status and being better educated, although the gap may now be closing. American journalists often mingle with leaders, particularly in the political arena, and consequently are suspected of belonging to an elite. Many are alert to the dangers of being coopted and adopt adversarial postures, perhaps in part to affirm their independence as well as to dig out the story.

The technique of establishing rapport may be less familiar than such styles of attack, but are even more important and often much more effective for in-depth journalism. David S. Broder, a skillful and friendly interviewer, induced hundreds of busy people to sit for long interviews and discussions. He wrote (in *Changing of the Guard*) that his "greatest debt is to the more than three hundred people who took time . . . for the rather lengthy interviews that provided the raw material for this book."[5]

Young leaders interviewed gave him more than the raw material he expected: they offered vision and hope. He found narrator Janet Brown outstanding, and noted that

[H]er disdain for mediocrity and her impatience with the *status quo* typify to me the spirit that she and her contemporaries bring to the challenge [of government and politics]. Like many of the others I met in writing this book, she made me feel better about the future.[6]

Broder's conclusions showed the reverse of the hard-bitten, cynical journalist-interviewer.

I feel some confidence that this generation has not lost its sense of direction or its capacity for leadership. On the big questions they have faced in their adult lives, their instincts have been more right than wrong . . .[7]

A combination of rapport, patience, and careful listening served Ben H. Bagdikian well in 1964 when he was preparing a story for the *Saturday Evening Post*. The topic was the likelihood of working-class Democratic districts voting for Barry Goldwater in the November presidential election as they had for George Wallace in the primaries. Bagdikian recalled:

I interviewed 200 voters in three cities. All began with positive statements about Goldwater, mostly about his implied criticism of Black activism and his toughness with the Russians. But by letting them talk at their own pace and direction, it became clear that they were much more worried about employment, social security and avoiding nuclear war, and they would end up voting for Lyndon Johnson, which they did. Had I taken their initial statements I would have been seriously misled, even though I did not try to influence their responses and they were being honest.[8]

The Cast of Characters and the Follow-up Question

Appropriate initial or follow-up questions that evoke desirable quotes depend on several factors for success. Probably the most important variable is the number of participants present. Lacey Fosburgh, in an unpublished letter to a student interviewer, considered what might happen in various settings: a large group such as a press conference; a small group of individuals each with a different concern; or the classic one-to-one interview. Discussing the small group interview, she showed how the presence of a number of people in the room made it harder for the interviewer to establish rapport with the narrator and to maintain control of the interview. The consequence was a shift that could not be reversed.[9] She was referring to the shift that occurs when the narrator seizes and holds control so that the interviewer cannot regain it. An aggressive narrator in effect uses the others in the room as an audience and can play to them, virtually relegating the interviewer to the status of an audience member. Once this happens it is hard for the interviewer to reestablish status as an equal, much less a controlling, player.

In general, formulating follow-up questions in a one-to-one interview depends on the ability to hear and understand what the narrator has said, and has not said. If more than two are present, the interviewer's alertness and rapport with the narrator can be dissipated, especially when other interviewers cause distractions with their own questions, or break concentration and continuity with sounds and movement.

The large press conference forestalls sequential questioning. The narrator commonly dominates the interviewers, choosing which queries to answer, which to ignore, and which to turn off with a joke. Usually only the brashest or the luckiest—or those the narrator sees as "safest"—manage to get follow-up questions asked and answered. (Note that press conferences—because of their size and nature—are not included in our definition of interviews, and are used here only for comparison and contrast.)

The Question Not Asked

A researcher combing an interview for useful material sometimes feels a small jolt, like missing a step on a flight of stairs. That sensation signals that something—the next logical question—is missing. Did the interviewer drop the ball? Did the narrator distract the interviewer, refuse to comment, or play coy? When an important question is not asked, the user feels the shock of disappointment and a sense of opportunity lost.

The researcher's regret can be matched by the chagrin of the narrator who has something significant to say but cannot work it in. The interviewer may insist on control, ignore the narrator's signals, and fail to pose the questions the narrator needs. There is a consequent danger that an interviewer or user may reach wrong or damaging conclusions based on assumptions or insufficient evidence. The interviewer's unfamiliarity with the facts and lack of preparation may well lead to inadvertent "fiction."

For example, journalist Ann Crittendon interviewed and wrote a profile of Bill Moyers in which he said she failed to question him on a key point related to damaging charges and hints that he was a malingerer. She stated that "Moyers managed to avoid another confrontation, at Lyndon Johnson's funeral, by having a false-alarm heart attack that fooled several doctors." She further reported that "one associate" (of Moyers) explained why Moyers did not want to attend the funeral.

In a "Letter to the Editor," "Moyers: For the Record," Moyers called the published statement an egregious error, identified his painful ailment as Tietze's Syndrome, and asked his doctor to issue a press release concerning his condition; this was done. Moyers wrote,

> If Ann had asked me about the matter, I would have told her what happened and shown her evidence to support me. She was misled by uninformed gossip.

He requested a retraction "because beguiling but untrue anecdotes like this can cause a man mischief for life." He also wrote,

> I am aghast that you and Ann would publish so serious a charge without at least having given me a chance to comment on it. Now, perhaps you can understand why I am reluctant to be interviewed for personality profiles.[10]

Moyers's own skill as an interviewer lends additional weight to the sense of injury he experienced as a narrator. Directly or by implication he dealt with three major points of technique: first, the interviewer did not ask him about the nature of his illness on the day of Johnson's funeral; second, she quoted an unnamed associate who made a damaging charge about Moyers's wish to avoid the funeral; and finally, she did not give him a chance to respond to the "associate's" charge. An alert editor could have noticed all three elements of the problem and given the narrator a chance for correction or rejoinder before publication. Afterwards, a correction or statement could have been issued in the columns of the magazine that printed the profile. Instead Moyers had to resort to the "Letters to the Editor" column to voice his complaint.

The Problem of Quotes: Off or On the Record

Journalistic interviewers deal with narrators who seek control, i.e., anonymity or protection, with respect to the use of what is said. In

Bagdikian's formulation these include (1) what was said is not to be used at all, "off the record"; (2) the material may be used, but the speaker is not to be cited as source, "not for attribution"; or (3) the material may be used for the interviewer's own information, "background." Quoting the narrator but not giving the name transforms the source from a real person into a faceless abstraction: "an observer," "an informed/highly placed source," or other character, avoiding both visibility and responsibility, and limiting possible adverse effects on the source. A narrator may also ask for anonymity in specific roles: as whistle-blower who may risk punishment for revealing wrong-doing, or as an advisor or administrator seeking to protect a policy-making position.

Information that seems to journalists, readers, and researchers appropriate for public perusal and debate may appear to top-level federal administrators to be unwise and even dangerous leaks. It follows that being quoted publicly could endanger the narrator's future participation in inner circles or councils where policies are shaped. One who leaks information may escape punishment, but risks loss of access and influence, and for this reason may grant interviews but with the proviso of anonymity. In a note to *The Price of Power*, Seymour Hersh reported that

> Dozens of American officials, ranging from NSC [National Security Council] aides to Nixon Administration ambassadors, were interviewed for the chapters dealing with the Middle East, but only a few officials agreed to be quoted by name — *not out of a lack of conviction or fear of retribution, but solely in an attempt to avoid losing any influence on policy making.*[11] [emphasis added]

The interviewer who agrees to provide anonymity may recognize the launching of a trial balloon and find the limitation worthwhile. The story or the narrator may be important enough to warrant giving up control, and may lead to clues for future stories. Another related motive may be the need to compete and the hope of scooping other reporters. It is the rare reporter who, like I. F. Stone, has the energy and the wit to avoid the plant and the hand-out, and dig up stories entirely from other sources.

Journalists are aware of the "Washington style" vis-à-vis any news agency. To a greater or lesser degree, presidential administrations cut down the availability of news and of access to people interviewers would like to question. A potential narrator may be prevented from speaking to the press or allowed to do so only in the presence of a designated official. In turn, an interviewer's acceptability may be governed by his or her level of perceived friendliness to the administration. As a consequence, interviewers are in effect forced into agreements not to disclose names and sources, because only through these agreements are they able to gain access to information.[12]

Beyond other considerations, the timing of a request to impose limitations is crucial. Practices and rationalizations differ, but an off-the-record request made before the interview begins is different from one delivered during the course of the session or at the end. The early request sets agreement between interviewer and narrator. Technically, if the interviewer is unwilling to accept the conditions, the interview procedure can stop. If the demand comes during or after the interview, the narrator wants to have it both ways: deliver the basic message, but control its use.

Getting the Quote and Naming the Source

When the interviewer can and does ask the right question(s), the narrator may be unwilling to be quoted or identified. In such circumstances Mary Ellen Leary preferred to find a way to quote directly and name the source. She noted, however, that the "practice of accepting news without revealing the source is growing." She also indicated that narrators who require their statements to be used for background only may change their minds later, especially when they begin to see the way the story is shaping up:

. . . if you come back and say, "May I quote you on this and this?" they'll say "Oh, of course," because it will fit into your context of the story you're building and be pertinent. Once they've made this kind of blanket, "Let me speak freely," then you can go back and get them to stand for a few sentences.[13]

In short, she learned how to get the quote, while still playing fair with the narrator, in an elegant demonstration of journalistic technique.

Fairness plus inventiveness elicited sensational information—with attribution—and gave Leary a "great scoop" about Johnnie Evans, a California legislator in the 50s. Evans sat on the committee that heard most of George McLain's controversial measures concerning the state's elderly. (McLain was the principal, most active, and most effective lobbyist for the elderly during the early post-World War II period.) Leary recalled that "Evans, having drinks with some guys, talked about having been out making speeches for McLain and traveling around the state" with him. He said the same thing in an interview with her. As she recalled,

I got Johnnie Evans . . . to tell it to me again and sign a byline story saying, "Yes, sure, I take money from McLain. I'm on his lecture circuit, and I've been doing this for years."[14]

The story appeared over the byline, "by Assemblyman John Evans as told to Mary Ellen Leary, in his own words." Leary required the verification of the byline because Evans's admissions were damaging both to him and to his lobbyist employer McLain. Perhaps the most significant aspect of Evans's behavior was his repeated willingness to recount the story, either not knowing or not caring about such issues as conflict of interest.

A Quote, A Paraphrase, or A Pastiche?

The direct quote and the paraphrase are complementary but serve different purposes in reporting interviews. The quote uses the narrator's spoken words. A paraphrase, however, may be more clear, pithy, and readable than a direct quote when a statement is replete with fumbles, hesitations, and backtracking. A well-edited quote can produce a few sentences, or even phrases, that capture the essence of an interview, and also produce pithy and telling statements.

Style and esthetics also influence decisions on when to paraphrase and when to quote directly. Presenting extensive quotes to ensure accuracy or completeness of information may actually lessen communication. The reader or eventual user may yawn at overlong quotes that provide less usable information than a brisk paraphrase and a few clear phrases, intelligently quoted.

It is, however, a serious lapse of technique to indicate a direct quote when the narrator did not say the words attributed, or worse still, has not been interviewed at all.

A classic case of reported interviews that never occurred can be found in Katherine A. Towle's oral history memoir. She recounted quotations and paraphrases of interviews attributed to her during the confusions of the Free Speech Movement, while she was dean of students at the University of California, Berkeley. She said that reporters who had not spoken to her at all, either face-to-face or by telephone, nevertheless wrote direct "quotes" or paraphrases in their newspaper stories. Referring to an interview by Wallace Turner, San Francisco correspondent for the *New York Times,* she said

I might add that Mr. Turner was the only correspondent of a major newspaper who ever bothered to interview me directly in all of those long, difficult months.[15]

To the question, "Of a major newspaper or of any newspaper?" she answered, "any newspaper."[16] She made it clear that Wallace Turner was the only newsperson who interviewed her during that period.

Knowing how to quote and when to paraphrase are significant aspects of an interviewer's technique. The pastiche, however, is a questionable technique at best. The pastiche, "a hodgepodge of borrowed elements," suggests the last resort of the failed interviewer, who does not get fresh information from the narrator or other usual channels, and resorts to various borrowings to make up a story. This practice may be acceptable at times to add detail, but is not acceptable if quotes and paraphrases are faked and unattributed as secondary sources. In Dean Towle's case errors were compounded in this way. A reporter who had never interviewed or spoken to her wrote up what purported to be an interview, complete with "quotes" that were nothing of the sort. Other reporters took these "quotes" at face value, and requoted them. In this way a pastiche was born. What did Dean Towle actually say? Only Wallace Turner and the *New York Times* knew for sure.

Finding the Sources, Checking, and Cross-Checking

Finding the best sources for quotations does not necessarily mean beginning at the top, as David Halberstam noted in his research for *The Best and the Brightest.*

It was people primarily in the second, third and fourth tier of government who were helpful in piecing together the play and the action, although finally several of the principals themselves began to cooperate.[17]

His 688-page book was largely the product of his own interviews, a full-time

effort that took more than two and a half years. He talked to people who
might be knowledgeable about the men, the events, the decisions.
In all I did some five hundred interviews . . . seeing some people
as many as ten times, checking and cross-checking as carefully as
I could.[18]

Halberstam's persistence and thoroughness suggest a combination of journalistic and scholarly research interviewing. Journalists working against daily or weekly deadlines could hardly return to an informant "as many as ten times," or amass the thousands of pages of notes Halberstam collected. Nevertheless the need for checking and cross-checking—to ensure accuracy— is a well-recognized principle.

With all the documents Halberstam read and cited, as a reporter he still relied heavily on interviews for his study of leaders and their decisions. The checking and cross-checking of the reporter who writes for daily or weekly publication forms the pattern; the work of the reporter on years-long projects differs more in scale and range than in principle and technique.

"Conversations With . . . " and Questions of Focus and Space

Sometimes the journalistic interviewer appears center stage, sharing the spotlight with the narrator, and at times even edging the latter into the wings. One technique that shifts the spotlight toward the interviewer is to combine an interview strategy of challenge with skepticism expressed in the written introduction to stories, or in long queries in published accounts. Anna Starcke, interviewing in South Africa, stated in her introduction to the published interview that "very little can be achieved with the present government set-up." In opening the interview she said to the narrator, then South Africa's Minister of Foreign Affairs, Roelof Frederik "Pik" Botha, "Minister, you must be a very frustrated man." She added, "I didn't expect an answer and I didn't get one. But he stared a long time out of the window. Not that I have fallen for Pik Botha's snow technique." She also cited Botha's "flair for drama" and "occasional hamming."[19] Thus a page and a half into the introduction, the reader finds several pejorative statements by the interviewer and only a wordless stare from the narrator who, of course, did speak up during the course of the interview.

The center-stage position appears in another of Starcke's interviews, which showed the narrator's answer (in Roman type) numbering only 13 lines, while the interviewer's queries and remarks (in Italic) numbered 27 lines.[20] Comparative length of question and answer is only one clue in evaluating the questioner's technique, but it does indicate the way the interviewer allocates prominence. By printing the full question, the interviewer does not necessarily imply that the reply is also full and complete. Further, the interviewer may later improve on the question, while the answer receives no such cosmetic attention. One may also suspect that interviewers who insist on unusual prominence and in fact have developed a kind of "name-interviewer" reportorial form, may also tend to dramatize the "fearless reporter" role at the expense of the persons being interviewed.

The apparent vogue for reporting journalistic interviews in unembellished question and answer form, as practiced by Oriana Fallaci, Starcke, and many others, can heighten the sense of dramatic interchange between interviewer and narrator and can seem to put the reader "in the room" during the interview. It also, however, introduces ambiguities and may prompt questionable assumptions. Questions and answers tend to look verbatim and imply publication of what was actually said although the material may have been edited, cut, and rearranged substantially.

Taunts and sarcasm can stimulate certain kinds of answers, possibly those preferred by the interviewer. Oriana Fallaci interviewing Federico Fellini went on the attack. She said, " . . . you are so withdrawing, so secret, so modest. . . . but it is our duty . . . for the sake of the nation. . . . " to discuss Fellini. She drew the retort: "Nasty fibber. Rude little bitch."[21]

It is only a step from stimulating the desired answer to virtually demanding it. Fallaci said to the late Ingrid Bergman (in a sequence that appeared essentially friendly): "Aren't you afraid of growing old? All women are afraid of growing old and if you tell me you're not I won't believe you." Bergman, who denied such fear, added, "But you must believe me."

Interviewing Anna Magnani, Fallaci diagnosed the actress as suffering from "immutable sadness masked by vivacity. . . . " Magnani responded, "Don't tell me you've come to make something sad and depressing of me? Today, too, when I'm happy; I've had a tax rebate. . . . " Later Fallaci insisted on "this painful irony of yours, the constant bitterness. . . . " while Magnani asked, "What are you driving at? What do you mean? And me feeling like a lizard in the sun. . . . What must I do to convince you that I'm cheerful . . .?"

These examples show the interviewer's presumption of superior wisdom and power that make the subject a supplicant, offering defenses and pleading for belief. But even when friendly, the interviewer's omniscience swerves into such oddities as an analysis of behavior and personality based on shoulder structure. Fallaci musing on Sean Connery observed his "excessive shoulders: the shoulders of a man who eats a lot, drinks a lot, makes love a lot."

Whether or not the reader gains a clear picture of Bergman, Magnani, or Connery, the clearest view is that of Fallaci. This provocative style shows the interviewer seeking sensation and shock value rather than an unbiased picture of the narrator. The burden is on the interviewer to be more interesting than the narrator, lest the reader or researcher become impatient and wish she would step aside and let others appear more clearly. The Fallaci technique appears to go beyond confrontation, which implies a rough equality. Instead the interviewer has become prosecutor, judge, and jury, and the narrator a defendant, and a muzzled one at that.

In "The Interview as Art" Wilfred Sheed recognized that narrators can turn the table, as he commented on issues of *Writers at Work: The Paris Review Interviews.* (This ongoing series of interviews, with the sixth published in 1984, uses the question-and-answer form. The interviewer takes the place of Q, and the author/narrator, A. Sheed himself wrote the introduction to the fourth series.)

Sheed's 1976 essay called the interviews "authors' contributions to their own gossip . . . their own fair copies of themselves . . . "[22] thus linking technique to control. Sheed's observation was fair comment but not fair criticism. The interviewers had explained the ground rules, and the narrators' control was made clear. Sheed may have expected a Fallaci-like domination and control by the interviewer, and felt disappointed when the *Paris Review* interviews tended toward scholarly techniques or at least gave narrators a measure of control.

In a later *Paris Review* series, an interview with Joyce Carol Oates included the following introductory explanation:

Many of the questions in this interview were answered via correspondence. She [Oates] felt only by writing out her replies could she say precisely what she wished to, without possibility of misunderstanding or misquotation.[23]

The Oates interview note suggested tactfully that while the author/narrator had some doubts about the interviewer, she also questioned her own ability to make herself understood.

In the introduction to the sixth series of interviews, Frank Kermode expanded on the ways individual authors exerted their control, in essence preventing the interviewer from exercising his or her technique.

Iris Murdoch . . . talked seriously but carefully rewrote everything she said before publication. Other writers prepare for the ordeal by deciding in advance what they will say, and again the sense of privileged talk is lost, and it becomes impossible for conversation to produce discoveries, as it should.[24]

Kermode's regretful note acknowledged that everyone behaved correctly, with the ground rules established and recognized; the interviewer could not be faulted, and the narrator was in control. The "interviewer," nevertheless felt let down. While nothing bad happened, the spark of discovery, the magic hadn't happened either.

Conversations, Dialogues, and Categories

"Conversations with . . . " or "Dialogues with . . . " as titles for interview collections can be intriguing but not fully informative. Definition and explanation in the text or the introduction can help the reader understand whether the conversations and dialogues are essentially journalistic, academic, research, or oral history-style sessions, or some original hybrid. (They are clearly not polling or survey research.) Readers can observe for themselves how prominent or even dominant the interviewer may be, but also may need information about such techniques as strictures on presentation, narrator approval, and control, as well as the eventual disposition of material.

Looking at a couple of examples reveals how well the editor helps the reader. Techniques tended to resemble those of oral history. *In Conversations with Writers II,* the introduction stated that interviewers gave the editors cassette tapes of interviews, with short biographical sketches of narrators, and brief descriptions of the interview settings. "The tapes were transcribed at . . .

the editorial office. Transcriptions were . . . sent to both interviewers and subjects [narrators] for approval before final editing." Significantly, the tapes "will become part of a permanent archive of oral history," although its identity and location are not stated.

The interviewer was identified in the work by the name "Conversations" in the question and answer style; the queries were brief and the focus stayed on the narrator. (On page 105, chosen at random in *Conversations,* the interviewer's comment occupied only one line; on the preceding page the interviewer had 9 lines of type, the narrator 26.)

Finally, the aim was "to provide a forum for leading authors by preserving their comments on their work and careers; to provide readers with insights . . . ; [and] an accurate image of writers as individuals."[25]

In *Constructing Policy: Dialogues with Social Scientists . . .* editor Irving Louis Horowitz described the enterprise as "not simply a series of interviews . . . but . . . a collective dialogue" that included follow-up interviews "to make sure that the final version represented the views held by each participant." Horowitz offered this careful presentation and its purpose "as a series of working interviews and exchanges that might someday provide a groundwork for a general theory of social science and public policy."[26] Although not entirely satisfied with the term "interviews," Horowitz used it again and again and seemed finally to accept it as an approximation of what he meant.

He signaled a rough equality between interviewer and narrator as the exchanges developed, although at times he as interviewer more than held his own with respect to argument and material. Sample pages (chosen at random and not necessarily representative) showed the following comparisons.

Printed Lines of Statement

Page No.	Interviewer	Narrator
13	16	25
14	8	33
22	34	8
26	43	0
	101	66

Keeping the questions short and encouraging longer answers is often a good rule of thumb in interviews; but Horowitz was developing dialogues in which he too could speak at length. He offered a useful insight into the differences in mind-set between the interviewer and the initiator of a dialogue. The examples, "Conversations," and "Dialogues," demonstrated slightly differing—but respectful—treatment of narrators. The conversations tended toward oral history technique, featuring narrator prominence and control. While the dialogues gave ample play to the narrator's words, they also featured a feisty, aggressive interviewer who competed at least as an equal, and who did not hesitate to speak at length.

Technique and Technology

The development of convenient tape recorders gave interviewers a tool that seemed designed to facilitate reporting and increase its accuracy. In fact, however, reviews on its performance are mixed. Edwin R. Bayley pointed out that it takes longer to produce a usable typed transcript from a tape than from good written notes.[27] As to reliability, it is not clear that the tape always "proves" what was actually said.

William B. Arthur, National News Council, noted that the council received complaints about the accuracy and fairness of quotations in newspapers. He expressed reservations about what tapes can prove, and how reliable they are as evidence.

> We have no way of knowing . . . what may have been left out, unless a person complaining submits a taping of the quoted material. And even then . . . tapes can be deceiving, or even doctored. . . . There are occasions when material readily available to the reporter is left out, resulting in a one-sided report when the other side could have been presented.[28]

As to basic use in documentation and verification, however, Arthur noted that:

> More and more reporters are taping their interviews . . . to insure accuracy and fairness, and more and more persons being interviewed are taping simultaneously for their own protection.[29]

Some journalistic interviewers are reluctant even to use a much older device, the telephone. While writers for the daily press find the phone indispensable as a time saver, interviewers who are under less pressure often reject it. In *The Powers That Be,* David Halberstam wrote: "By and large I do not like using the phone for magazine and book reporting . . . there is too little sense of the other person."[30]

Lacking a sense of the other person can be a serious disadvantage to an interviewer who relies on eye contact and observing body language and facial expressions for communicating, conveying nuances of meaning, and establishing rapport. The same can be true of the narrator who may prefer to know first-hand the kind of person asking questions, and who finds little help in a disembodied voice.

In short, technology may at times interfere with trust. Further, technology does not necessarily guarantee accuracy. It can lend itself to careless or deliberate misuse: telephone conversations can be recorded without mandatory warning beeps, tapes can be spliced, altered, and rerecorded. On the other hand, when used prudently and ethically, technology can foster efficiency and accuracy. The point is to recognize when and how technology can help; and to identify situations where older systems of note taking may be more effective and less distracting.

SURVEY RESEARCH:
CONSTRUCTING DATA

From the journalistic interview, we turn to the exacting and more restrictive technique of survey research and polling. The survey research interview is highly structured and questions are developed and prescribed beforehand. The interviewer is anonymous, and the respondent's identity is not reported (although it may be recorded in code if follow-up is permitted). This care safeguards privacy. The interviewer's options are both limited and supplemented by the telephone and the computer, now joined together in computer-aided telephone interviewing (discussed below).

Survey research and polling, the most impersonal of interview forms, follow conventions as rigid as those of the Noh play. The interviewer virtually wears a mask concealing approval or disapproval, and is trained to recite the questions as worded and in the prescribed order, without variation in inflection or emphasis. It is also useful to consider the respondent—across the table or at the other end of the telephone line—and observe possible consequences of these methods for the supplier of information.

Focus on Examples

In the examples we see conscientious pollsters and survey research interviewers striving to achieve statistical reliability, and to avoid bias, inaccuracy, and respondents' loss of anonymity. Formality, restrictions, controls, and lack of variation characterize this planned and blueprinted type of interview. In searching for reliability, however, some interviewers also show their concern about consequences of compression: the danger of losing data as well as various human values.

The Necessities of Survey Research

The better human interactions are understood, the more sophisticated survey research techniques become. For example, knowing that respondents may wish to please the interviewer or win approval, the questioner must maintain a neutral tone. Since the wording of a question may also suggest what is acceptable, survey designers try to avoid giving such signals (unless it is the sort of survey that is deliberately constructed to provide the desired answers). The sequence of questions can also have the effect of "leading" a respondent. For that reason, once the least value-laden sequence is determined, it does not vary. The entire interviewing effort aims at maintaining consistency and avoiding uncontrolled variations in the posing of questions and recording of answers.

Many research-oriented polls are designed to be accurate and reliable and to provide the best possible snapshot of respondents' views at the time. This is not to suggest, however, that polling and survey research are always value free. Some are designed to achieve a desired end, such as a candidate's own published polls, which may be intended to make him or her look like a winner.

Here, however, the unrigged polls and surveys and their techniques engage our attention. Despite variations and oddities that remain, polls and surveys have seen extraordinary improvements in the past few decades. The best of them hold up a mirror to society, showing views of current reality that we might not otherwise recognize.

Survey research interviewing is shaped by its procedures and the nature of its desired product. Research directors should "never forget that the study design must coordinate questionnaire construction and interviewer instruction with the coding and data-analysis operations."[31] Further, in public opinion polling, survey research generally responds to the same kinds of deadline pressures as the journalistic interview.

The quest for totals dominates both the purpose and analysis of survey results. One person's answers are not significant per se; totals are. Where questioners in other interview styles are free to be spontaneous or to adjust the wording and question sequence for each narrator, survey research rigorously excludes such options. Differences among research interviewers must be minimized or eliminated; respondents' answers need to be tallied comparably so they can fit into appropriate categories that translate into statistics.

The device of open-ended questions, however, can broaden the nature of responses. Such questions serve a variety of purposes. In the book *Hard Choices,* Kathleen Gerson explained the development of the question schedule used for the women in the study: It "gradually assumed the form of a life history questionnaire that guided the respondents through their personal 'life lines' and focused on mobility routes through work and family events." She added that

> The final interview schedule was structured to guide the interview and ensure comparability across groups; it was open-ended to allow for *probing* and *discovery of the range of possible answers* and to accommodate *new theoretical insights* as they occurred.[32] [emphasis added]

The pairing of control to maintain comparability with openness to new insights demonstrates one way interviewers/researchers in survey research can work to minimize its intrinsic limitations.

Techniques and Options—Avoiding Bias

As noted earlier, project directors and interviewers establish and maintain control of the interviews and avoid variations. To do so, they focus on the best ways to formulate and administer questions. Schuman and Presser have listed several of the options in techniques basic to survey research:

- open vs. closed (fixed-response) questions

- encouragement or discouragement of "don't know" responses

- presence or absence of middle alternatives in questions

- balanced vs. unbalanced questions ("Do you favor or oppose this law?" vs. "Do you favor this law?")

- variations in question order and in the order of alternatives within questions

- changes in tone of wording

- variations in measuring the strength of attitudes[33]

With respect to wording, Schuman and Presser judged obvious bias the least harmful because it is most easily recognized, whereas the harder-to-spot "more subtle changes in wording . . . can have large effects on responses." Further, researchers often need to compare results of two or more surveys in seeking evidence of trends, but are frustrated if question wording and sequence are not identical. The order within a questionnaire can produce a "context effect" that is hard to control, even when the same question is asked in different surveys. Schuman and Presser cautioned:

There is probably no such thing as a perfectly unbiased survey question . . . no matter how skilled and well-intentioned the researcher [research director] may be. It is now widely recognized that bias in wording cannot be separated from the goals of a study and the interpretation of the resulting data.[34]

Thus the researcher looking for "evidence" in survey research and polling can both observe the ways the interviewer avoids bias and maintains control, and recognize that an "irreducible" margin for error probably exists in even the most thoughtful and expertly conducted survey research and polling.

In a recent analysis, sociologist Richard P. Appelbaum of University of California, Santa Barbara, questioned the sampling and other methods used by the US Department of Housing and Urban Development in a survey of homelessness in the US. He saw flaws in the use of materials, and also commented that discussion of possible sampling bias should be included in the report of the HUD study findings. The UC *Clip Sheet* reported him as saying that HUD officials refused to provide information needed to analyze their methodology, alleging that the information was privileged. Further,

Appelbaum's own investigation indicated that HUD failed to interview some of the nation's top experts on homelessness and failed to include in its report the information supplied by those experts it did interview.[35]

He suggested several problems with technique: failure to discuss problems of sampling bias, faulty editorial judgment concerning choice of respondents for scholarly research interviews, and questionable choices on what to cut and what to include.

The "Right Question" and Time to Listen

The narrator as citizen must have formulated a personal view—an informed opinion—of public issues before he or she can give a response that is more than superficial to the political survey researcher or pollster. Ben H. Bagdikian argued, however, that we as citizens "have accepted far too much the expression of public issues as defined by candidates," and as a consequence most of the public gets "a pretty poor education" in political matters. As a result, a narrator's deepest concerns may not be available at the level of quick response or adequately tapped by pre-set questions. Bagdikian said that

if you ask the right questions and if you listen long enough, you begin to hear the deep concerns of different groups of citizens, worries and expectations that are profound and on which they must act politically with only the most marginal clues from their candidates.[36]

An interview that provides time for the interviewer to listen, time to establish rapport, and the ability to rephrase and direct questions is outside the realm of survey research and polling. While a journalist may accept a quick answer and a "quotable quote," persistence and interest can evoke a deeper response in journalistic, as well as scholarly research and oral history interviews.

Survey research and polling nevertheless offer appropriate techniques for a different purpose: the quick response of a representative sample, reflecting current impressions, however they may have been formed. The snapshot in time does show the surface with greater efficiency than any other interview style. The deeper concerns that are harder for the narrator to formulate and even harder to express emerge to reward the interviewer who can use techniques that allow more time for questioning and listening.

The problem that remains is how to bring the deeper concerns on public issues into closer correlation with the choices posed by candidates and ballot measures. Where the quick answers of polling mirror campaign slogans, the circle of communication can close without attending to the issues of greatest significance.

Telephone Interviewing and Polling

Our picture of the interview—two people seated in a room, one questioning and one answering—is undergoing change. Now technology may intervene to link them by telephone, either close by or at some distance from each other. Particularly in the case of survey research and polling, the interviewer is likely to sit at a central location where supervisors can monitor interviews.

The writer suggested to pollster Mervin D. Field that it would be easier for an interviewer to establish rapport with a respondent if the two could see each other in person, rather than having to rely on the voice only, as in a telephone interview. Field replied that was no longer true, and that "phone rapport" is easier to establish than rapport in person. Phone calls may overcome the reluctance associated with opening one's door to a stranger, and long distance calls may quiet fears that a caller might be checking to see if anyone is at home.

Further, a neutral, pleasant, disembodied voice on the phone carries fewer clues to age, origin, color, or other personal characteristics that might cause a reaction in the person being interviewed. Thus in his survey research (90 percent of his work) and in polling (10 percent), Field saw the phone interview as the technique of choice both for maximizing interviewer efficiency and for avoiding anxieties and distractions on the part of the respondent.[37]

A recent development is CATI (computer-assisted telephone interviewing), whereby interviewers read from a computer screen—cathode ray tube (CRT)—that displays in sequence the questionnaire programmed for the survey. The interviewer reads questions from the screen word for word in the order prescribed, and speaks with respondents through telephone headsets. To record each answer, the interviewer depresses keys on the terminal keyboard. Such immediate recording minimizes variations in tallies and recording. In addition, the process saves time, and the data can be computed and ready for use virtually as soon as the last interview is completed.[38]

Field has called the CATI system the wave of the future for surveying large samples. He cited the system's efficiency, fast turn-around, and ready availability of results as well as the capacity for "lots of branching" that allows a response to be followed with alternative queries that lead to additional choices.[39]

Interview, Questionnaire, and Intercept

The "mall intercept" survey method is designed to capture the attention of persons at a time when they may be responsive or in a buying mood. Interviewers approach individuals in shopping malls, inviting them to fill out questionnaires and to take part in interviews. In addition, respondents may receive self-administered questionnaires by mail or by hand, to be completed and returned to the interviewers by mail later.

Where speed and proportion of response are important, questionnaire-interview combinations completed on the spot out-perform those entrusted to respondents and the mail. As compared to the CATI system, the latter provides a self-contained interview at maximum speed, avoids repeated handling of questionnaires, or waiting for mail delivery. The mall intercept capitalizes on timing, the sociability of an outing, and the ability to combine techniques. It comes full circle back to the face-to-face interview.

The Restive Respondent

Questions and ideas for improvement in survey research methods center on two issues: the quality of the data yield for the interviewer, and the response, attitude, and satisfaction of the narrator.

Surveys accomplish their mission when they succeed in establishing control, quantification, and comparability of information. This outcome pleases the interviewer. At the same time, survey researchers recognize that respondents may not be pleased at all by the process or the product. Converse and Schuman expressed concern about the ways the tight controls of survey research techniques affect the respondents, and observed

the common complaint, that closed questions render very imper-
fectly certain respondents' thought and generate considerable
respondent dissatisfaction.[40]

Interviewers recognize that it is hard to approach a fair rendering of narrators'
thoughts in any interview style, and harder still to fit a multi-edged opinion
smoothly into the round hole of the survey tally. Questions must be simplified
and answers often oversimplified to fit the system: inevitably refinements and
nuances are brushed aside; further, an annoyed respondent may grumble that
the carefully wrought questions were the "wrong" questions. If much of a
respondent's satisfaction arises from communication, a feeling of noncom-
munication brings the opposite.

Converse and Schuman took such complaints seriously, and in response
urged systematic collection of data, presumably to guide efforts at improving
the system.[41]

A literature review by Sudman and Bradburn found general agreement
that "The research interview . . . does not directly affect the respondent's
needs or interests," particularly since the interviewer primarily determines
"the purposes, the rules of behavior, and the limits of the relationship."[42]

The respondent may seek in vain for a reward: there is little satisfaction
in answering when the tallied answer is not quite what the speaker meant to
say, and not much reward in a structure imposed by the requirements of the
interviewer and unresponsive to those of the respondent. If the session should
prove interesting, the respondent may want to talk further with the interviewer, or to elaborate on a question. Unfortunately, the rules are not geared
to permit such responses and individuality.

The urge to simplify and standardize extends to social scientists' work
with survey data, as Grimshaw noted, while he expressed concern at the "aim
to eliminate the variability of human response in order to standardize." He
also urged that when researchers collapse data to fit into manageable
categories, they should make such procedures explicit. In this way they could
facilitate recovery of "lost data," and improve the evaluation and interpretation of the findings.[43] The "variability of human response" that respondents
prize also offers value to researchers, although they may seek to minimize it.
Grimshaw suggested that more sophisticated methods of establishing
categories, and of tracking lost data could regain these values for researchers,
and perhaps convert what has been pared away into a usable resource.

These examples suggest that both researchers and respondents sometimes have cause for complaint, but the following suggests that picture is not
wholly one-sided for respondents.

Possible Rewards

Converse and Schuman also recognized some potential benefits:

The interview can offer the respondent values that may be missing
in much ordinary conversation: (1) attentive listening; (2) con-

sideration of the personal and experiential; (3) expression of controversial opinions without risk of argument or disapproval; and (4) intellectual stimulation and insight . . . [44]

Thus they suggested that respondents in survey research can enjoy some rewards similar to those experienced to varying degrees in other interview styles.[45]

Multiple Languages

Language as a basic element of interview technique is largely taken for granted, although survey research is particularly sensitive to the power of word choice, word order, and the use of specific terms. Most survey research in the US is of course conducted in English, but we need to recognize the significance of non-English-speakers and the use of other languages in multilingual communities.

Mervin D. Field noted that surveys require "reachable" populations for respondents in various "markets"—political, business, or social. Communication is accomplished through language—if not English, then some other. A valid sample of the "social market" in the San Francisco Bay Area, for example, would include some long-term immigrants and visitors as well as newcomers and more recent refugees. At present, however, not all of these persons would be part of the "political" or "business" markets.

Some learn English quickly, some at a slower pace, and some not at all. While many bilingual respondents do move into the mainstream of language, Field noted that even when questionnaires have been translated for Spanish-speakers, some who speak both languages will choose to handle the answers in English.[46]

Others who do not know English or who are less confident need different language options. Consequently, multilingual interviewers and questionnaires for some time to come may be a valuable means of reaching varied groups in American survey research. It follows that a working knowledge of more than one language—or reliance on translators—becomes an integral part of the researcher's technique.

Conclusion

The respondent is not only a source of data, but also an individual with interests and feelings that need to be addressed through the politics of the interview. With respect to survey tools, it is still unclear how best to balance quantitative analysis in survey research with protection for qualitative values. To reduce interviewer control, rigor, and comparability of data could threaten the validity of the findings. If survey research must be relatively uniform and numerically oriented, perhaps those limitations need to be accepted. Enrichment and interpretation may more properly lie in the development of freer techniques, and other interview styles that might supplement or accompany the survey.

Besides its "pure research" aspects, survey research and polling are valuable for testing researchers' hypotheses, for raising the consciousness of narrator groups, and a variety of other purposes. One prominent function is political polling and its link with the media, an association we now address.

UNEASY LINK:
POLITICAL POLLING AND THE PRESS

The relationship between polling and the media commands attention for two reasons. First, poll results—as circulated by the media—can exert dramatic influences on political processes. Second, the media's role is shifting from that of critic to proprietor, as some of the media bring polling under their own auspices and control. The point is not to raise suspicions about the integrity of the media or the polls, but to note a vertical concentration of power that bears watching.

Focus on Examples

Political polls often make news; the press needs news, polls need users, and newspapers use polls. Such symbiotic relationships are not intrinsically good or bad, but our examples raise the question of what happens when one partner (the press) takes over the other (the polls) and does the polling itself.

When the power of the polls and the press combine, the result can propel some candidates to victory and slow the progress of others. Such power requires skill, prudence, and objectivity in interpreting and printing poll results. The examples show the ways pollsters and the press have sought to work out their relationships. Finally, the examples raise but fail to answer the question of whether and to what extent the combination of polls and press can and do produce what the public needs to know.

Interpreting for the Interpreters

Each survey and polling interview is only a single component of the collective final product, awaiting processing and interpretation before the information is usable. In contrast, journalistic, scholarly research, and oral history interviews can convey their messages individually and at times directly to the reader, needing no elaborate intermediary process. So massive is the harvest of survey research and polling, however, that it appears to be prompting growth of an auxiliary industry designed to aid poll interpreters and users.

A 1981 promotional mailing from the journal *Public Opinion* stated that "every issue is packed with 20 pages of 'Opinion Roundup' . . . a choice collection of as many as *70 revealing public opinion polls."* [emphasis in the original] In addition,

> Many columnists have found quotable material in our pages,
> among them George Will, David Broder, Tom Wicker, Evans &
> Novak, John Roche, Pat Buchanan, Charles Bartlett, Allan Otten.
> . . . Articles from PUBLIC OPINION have been reprinted on the
> most important editorial pages in the country . . . *The Washing-*
> *ton Post*, the *Chicago Tribune*, the *San Francisco Examiner, The*
> *Christian Science Monitor, The Wall Street Journal*, and else-
> where.[47]

Though claims of widespread quotation are familiar, the emphasis on poll
material is notable. In addition, publisher William J. Baroody, Jr., saw the
magazine as helping "a broad, general audience understand the meaning of
the vast mountains of opinion poll data,"[48] presumably by interpreting the
mountain down to manageable size. He appeared to be warning nonexpert
readers that unaided they could not hope to transform the quantities of data
into useful information, but need help from the media—either his publication
or others that may well use its interpretations. Ironically, the individual poll
respondents who contributed to this overwhelming mass of data would need
to have the results interpreted, like everyone else. As more layers of the
"priesthood" step forward to interpret the mysteries of surveys to the common folk and their leaders, the surveys appear to take on oracular powers,
even though practitioners assure us that polls and surveys should not be seen
as truth or revelations of the future, but merely as "snapshots in time."

Power of Polling: Hypnosis and Prediction

Readers like to believe media reporters and interviewers are alert and
knowing, especially in their reporting on polls. In the November 1974 gubernatorial election in California Jerry Brown and Houston Fluornoy were the
leading candidates, featured in floods of reports on their standing in the political polls. In the early polling and through the campaign, Brown led. As the
campaign neared its close, however, the polls revealed a sharp turn in public
opinion in favor of Fluornoy; the polls found it, but the press did not report
that change. Mary Ellen Leary said it is "impossible to say how much reporters became hypnotized by the polls . . . inevitably showing Brown in the
lead." She observed that there was the "journalistic failure to discern a sharp
change . . . in the public mind in the last ten days of October."[49] Further,
Mervin D. Field had contended earlier that "whether they realized it or not,
the media followed the public in accepting polls as predictions."[50]

Because of deadline pressures, Field telephoned the results of his last
poll (November 1, 1974) to the *Los Angeles Times,* rather than mailing it. His
polls had found the sharp change and reported it to the paper. Field recalled
that he had talked to the rewrite desk and thought he had "put the focus on
Fluornoy's gain." The news story, however, relegated that finding to the
second paragraph, and emphasized Brown's "substantial lead."[51] Thus even
the respected *Los Angeles Times,* with both the Field poll and its own poll,
plus a record of reporting fully on California politics, apparently missed the
significance of the change.

Snapshots, Blackouts, and Consequences for Candidates

What do polls on political issues and candidates tell the researcher? First, according to Field, polls "can provide snapshots in time, some understanding of how people are reacting to what's going on." He regarded the individual polls as superficial, but capable of setting the stage so the media presumably could develop more substantive material.[52] In short, the snapshots can affect the information diet of readers and viewers.

Second, polling results can "black out" the candidates of legitimate minority parties as well as write-ins. Rollin Post, TV political commentator, expressed concern about the media's failure to cover contestants who do not appear in polls as front-runners. He said, "I simply don't know how to distribute coverage other than on the basis of the polls and yet I feel this measurement is in many ways unfair."[53]

In *Phantom Politics*, Leary's evidence supported Post's observations. She noted further that a candidate's showing of relative poll strength or popularity influenced his or her ability to buy advertising, which in turn depended on the ability to raise campaign funds. Funds flow to front-runners, in something of a self-fulfilling prophesy.

Commenting on California's 1974 gubernatorial election, Leary called the candidates' coverage "tailored to poll status," and traced the way the press functioned as a "curious link in the cycle."

Newspaper stories became evidence to potential contributors of a candidate's significance. But a candidate's news value depended upon his poll standing, which depended upon his television spots, which depended upon his fund-raising, which depended upon his getting into the newspapers . . . and *that* depended on his poll standing.[54] [emphasis in original]

To the extent that a candidate's standing in the polls is shaped by what the sampled voter-respondents say, those views at snapshot time carry considerable weight. As Warren Miller noted

We've gone away from a reliance on the politician as political informant, who can in turn then tell the readers. . . . Instead we've gone to a much greater emphasis on the *voter*.

The voter is playing a larger role in all phases of the election process from nomination through election day. The techniques, the methods of public opinion polling, make it possible to follow that participation.[55] [emphasis in the original]

Miller's view is in many ways a hopeful one, that polling enhances the voter's role. Yet polling itself can only provide an interview style and technique; the voter-respondent must be the source of content. Content and technique combine to shape the value of the response.

In Bagdikian's analysis, the interviewer/respondent partnership requires the interviewer to take time to listen for underlying concerns and ask the right questions, and the respondent to possess enough information to give meaningful rather than empty answers. With such potent variables at work, Miller's statement that the voter is playing a larger role appears to be value-free. He does not imply that the role is necessarily well played, that the players are well informed, or that the outcome is good or bad. Polling is a powerful tool that demands expertise of the interviewer as well as poise and knowledge by the respondent in order to achieve a product with more than superficial meaning.

The New Pollsters and the Triumph of the Telephone

Newspapers, magazines, and broadcast networks have joined the race to conduct or commission public polls that often use the telephone. E. J. Dionne Jr., writing in the *New York Times,* noted that sampling methods have "won telephone surveys a reputation for accuracy that rivals . . . in-person interviews." Since polling by phone costs much less than face-to-face interviews, "the triumph of the phone has encouraged smaller newspapers and television stations—along with smaller entrepreneurs—to try their hand at surveys." In a compilation of 147 polls listed by a CBS News unit, 43 were established from 1978 to 1980. The 147 were "state and regional polls conducted by local newspapers or broadcast outlets around the country."[56]

Dionne presented two quotes that highlighted some pros and cons of such polling. On the positive side, Douglas L. McKnight, executive producer of special projects for KGO-TV (San Francisco) called "A vote . . . a simple declarative sentence . . . " whereas polls "can get the rest of the paragraph." On the other hand, Albert H. Cantril, chair of the National Council on Public Polls, noted the proliferation of polling as tending to "feed the presumption that all numbers are equal." Dionne said, "some numbers are more reliable than others, and all numbers can be either enlightening or misleading depending on how they are used."[57]

The expansion of polling and its use by the media bring survey research and polling directly into the orbit of journalism. The linking of roles and techniques prompts some questions: Does this development further concentrate power within the media? Or does proliferation offer greater variety and room for choice, when power is distributed among a variety of polls? Does it matter who does the polling? Does the tendency toward vertical concentration serve the public interest in promoting public information and understanding?

Proliferation of polls is one phenomenon; the growth of polling by the media is part of the groundswell, but both pose a distinctive question. "Who will watch the watchers?"

In-House Press Polls

Irreverence and skepticism bordering on the cynical are often considered hallmarks of American journalism. The best journalists question, doubt, and often find fault—particularly with the performance of public officials—as the interviewers push for better and more revealing answers. On the other hand, media critics are taken aback when the press avoids the aggressive questioning that might have revealed Watergate in its early stages, or fails to develop a challenging analysis to apply to the Reagan administration's social, economic, and fiscal policies.

Similarly, while press skepticism should also be expected in discussions of survey research and polling results, it is not clear to what extent the press will challenge polls commissioned and paid for by the newspapers or the TV stations themselves. It is also unclear whether the placement of poll results on front pages or burial among the grocery ads will be determined by significance and validity, or by other criteria. Richard Reeves has noted ruefully,

> I was the chief political correspondent of the *New York Times* when we commissioned our first poll. We placed all those results on page one because they had cost us $80,000 and I needed to show my bosses that those expensive results were worth page one display.

He added,

> Any institution, be it a television network or a newspaper, will feature heavily what they have an investment in. The people who decided to make that investment are going to try to make themselves look as if they spent the company's money wisely.[58]

Need for Analysis and Interpretation

Warren Miller saw the major transformation in the area of polling and the media as "moving the research enterprise in-house." Consequently those engaged in the "new mode of reporting" must make the effort to understand the literature in the field and also develop an understanding of both academics and practitioners in politics. He noted that skilled person-power is the basic tool of public opinion research and that it "takes a lot of money from the paper or the radio station"; but that the "real major problem is the substantive understanding of . . . [what] is being reported." In the absence of knowledge and understanding on the part of the reporter who is writing polling results, he thought, "you might as well simply commission any of the syndicated polls, and let them tell you about the interpretation, the important questions."[59]

Thus the reporter who interprets in-house media polls, and the editor who determines their prominence and play, will determine whether the move in-house gives the public more of what it needs, or less.

In-House Polls: Narrowing the Scope

Additional problems of in-house polls relate to restrictions on timing and content. One can speculate that since "newness" does not necessarily imply importance and all that is important is not necessarily news, the quest for newsworthiness may prompt papers to narrow both the time-span and the range of topics covered by in-house polls. Underlying factors in public problems and long-term developments, whose discussion would benefit from a longer track-record of polling, may not find a place in the press's own polls. When a crisis erupts, polling makes news, but that timing cannot serve the needs of seasoned readers or problem-solvers who seek earlier warnings and longer-term polling results to provide greater depth and reveal long-term trends.

Similarly, experienced pollsters and survey researchers may recognize broader areas of concern than those dictated by the immediate needs of the press. If pollsters' judgments are not followed, poll results may be the poorer. In-house conduct of polls may restrict the diet of tips, clues, and alerting ideas on which good journalism thrives, since effective pollsters are often aware of emerging problems and attitudes whose early recognition can be of significant value to the investigative press. Journalists need all the ideas they can get; many they find for themselves, but they also need the stimulus of the additional ideas and views the independent pollsters can offer.

From the techniques and concerns of survey research and polling and of journalism, we turn now to the second pair of interview types: scholarly research interviews and oral history interviews.

SCHOLARLY RESEARCH AND CHECKING BACK

Interviewers' checking or calling back to verify facts or interpretations, and/or the review of drafts by narrators, comprise a technique so central to one type of scholarly interview as to be its distinguishing characteristic. The scholarly and the oral history interview both provide prime examples of the check-back. (The oral history interview is entirely subject to the narrator's approval.) Checking back—in these two styles—means that the interviewer or editor submits to the narrator a written account of what was said. The narrator reviews and sometimes rewords and corrects copy to assure the accuracy of the information, and the acceptability of both the narrative and the quotes as submitted for publication.

In this connection, Mary Ellen Leary observed that the press is moving toward a magazine-type of approach, which involves the journalistic interviewer in more checking back with narrators than was the case formerly. This newer approach is applied especially to technical fields, e.g., stories on scientific or legal matters.

Some Examples in Academic and Oral History Interviews

Both scholarly research and oral history interviews demonstrate the need for the narrator's consent, approval, and confidence; neither type confronts the intense time pressures evident in the other styles of interviews. Scholarly interviewers do recognize, however, the importance of scheduling and timing as intrinsic aspects of technique, and of the narrator's readiness and willingness to participate. (Timing can also be a concern when narrators' review is long-drawn-out, or project advisors must be sought out for consultation.)

Oral history interviewers illustrate the need for knowledge and preparation; stimulation of narrators' memories; the significance of rapport; and the values of silence. Finally we observe ways oral history and its techniques may be useful to professionals in other fields.

A Closer Look at Scholarly Research Interviews

Checking back comes near the end of the interview process. Project planning comes first, followed by the training and supervision of interviewers, choice of question areas, selection of narrators, and judgments on scheduling.

Interviewers and researchers use factual information to develop leading questions, but allocate interview time for the open-ended queries that may reveal additional insights. Most narrators have taken part in or closely observed the activities under study; they are bearers of information or interpretations that otherwise would not be generally available until some time in the future, if at all. Their statements often provide current, first-hand accounts.

Further, scholarly research interviews concerning private or public organizations can fill information gaps. The interviews may provide material where minutes, notes, or annual reports are not available. They can also include information on background discussion and informal negotiations that are not usually captured even where formal records are kept.[60]

Control and Self-Control as Technique

An interviewer must exert some control even when the narrator is highly qualified and sometimes high-powered. This means that the interviewer draws upon a high level of background information, plus attentiveness, freedom from bias, and avoidance of blind spots. An interviewer's blind spot can block out a promising lead even though the narrator sends clear signals. On the other hand, an interviewer needs judgment and tact to prevent trivialities from dominating the session and causing significant material to be slighted.

If the interviewer's skills are unequal to the task, a session may decline into irascible needling that annoys the narrator, minimizes productivity, and reduces chances for future interviews. The narrator who is at ease and sees a purpose in the interview is more likely to keep the door open for the future; a disappointed narrator may find ways to slam it shut. Finally, it goes almost without saying that the interviewer explains and honors all commitments to submit drafts for review and accept corrections offered.

Timing as Technique, and Number of Reviews

Stanley Scott has experimented with and used scholarly interviews to support research and writing on such California policy issues as seismic safety and the governance of the San Francisco Bay Area and of the coast. His observations provide the basis for much of the following discussion.[61]

Since Scott sought "current thinking" for his book on coastal governance, he could not wait for popular publications and the scholarly literature to emerge. Therefore, the interview program proved essential. His book on California's coast and coastal commissions offered insight into the way the interview system worked with more than a hundred persons, including many who gave "formal, in-depth interviews."

Another hundred commented in discussion and correspondence on the same topics. Individual narrators reviewed their own quotes. Further, both the first and second drafts of the book—incorporating quoted excerpts from interviews—were circulated extensively for comment and criticism. Many sections were reworked into third and fourth drafts that were circulated for further review and comment. The final draft benefitted from the opinions of

> coastal commissioners and staff, concerned environmentalists, land-owners and would-be developers, other affected business and labor organizations, interested staff of both the [California state] legislative and executive branches, and a variety of other parties and observers.[62]

Thus the check-back and overall review included narrators who could evaluate the treatment of their own interviews, as well as of different interpretations, plus reviews by other persons whose contributions were not in interview form.

A strategy on timing is crucial for scholarly interviews. (This aspect of timing is to be distinguished from the long process of checking back and reviewing; it has to do with whether to interview in January or June or to interview this year or two years from now.) As in the coastal governance book, check-back interviews are well suited for scholarly use in monitoring rapidly changing political and governmental developments. Scott said that it is in fact difficult to study ongoing processes without interviews. On the other hand, he noted that fitting available interview time and funds to support the project with the on-rush of events is a major problem.

The techniques of interview scheduling and the timing of questions present opportunities and pose hazards. The researcher may have funds and trained interviewers available and want to put them to work. They can, however, be virtually wasted on material that is in the process of losing timeliness and being superseded. In addition, the scholarly researcher remains aware of the budget in relation to the fiscal year. Since funds made available in a specified year often cannot be held over for a more convenient time, circumstances may force decisions to use the funds prematurely or lose them. As a consequence, interview funds may already have been spent before the time is really ripe, when concepts and developments have reached their most significant phase.

This brief summary of the scholarly research interview leads to consideration of the oral history interview.

ORAL HISTORY:
SERVING THE NARRATOR AND THE FUTURE

Why do oral history narrators agree to grant interviews? Willa K. Baum suggested that it is in part to "make concrete one's experience and wisdom and to . . . [create] from them a heritage to hand down to one's family and communal heirs." An oral history, however, must be more than a mere "recording of unfocused reminiscences" or "rambling conversations"; these would satisfy neither narrator nor interviewer, nor for that matter the readers and researchers of the future. Thus a narrator's thoughtful recollections, plus the interviewer's skill and "knowledge of the whole historical context of the person's life," are needed to produce material of lasting value.[63]

The Interviewer: Focus and Preparation

The oral history interviewer needs to become familiar with facts and other information to understand the narrator, the era, and the events of the individual's life. The reminiscences require focus, so the interviewer usually gives the narrator an outline and/or series of queries to help jog memory and elicit maximum information. In the system used at the Regional Oral History Office of The Bancroft Library both participants have at least this kind of basic outline before them during the sessions. The narrator, however, is usually free to depart from the outline, to add or delete items, or select topics to develop in the interviews.

Major exceptions are certain tightly controlled interviews in a topic-focused series such as the Goodwin Knight-Edmund G. Brown, Sr., California gubernatorial project. A narrator would be asked to concentrate on experiences that occurred while he or she occupied a designated post or played a role, eg., as superintendent of public instruction, and informed that the session could devote a limited period to that topic.

In an interesting parallel, Harriet Zuckerman reported on "Interviewing an Ultra-Elite," i.e., Nobel laureates. While the interviews were clearly not oral history interviews, they showed similarities in the interviewer's research and preparation and in the narrators' responses. Zuckerman noted that "Every interview was preceded by intensive and detailed preparation by the [interviewer] investigator." This included a "summary of each laureate's career and his work . . . "[64] Although essential for the interviewer, these guides apparently were treated casually by the narrators, who made little use of them.

Zuckerman observed nevertheless that her own "Intensive preparation facilitated . . . interviewing . . . [and] gave evidence of the seriousness of the interviewer," thus establishing her status in the eyes of the narrators. Further, she was confident that her preparation provided questions that "called forth responses that would otherwise not have been elicited."[65] The benefits she recognized comprise the reward of the well-prepared interviewer in many styles: scholarly research, journalism, or oral history.

In some circumstances, of course, interviewing technique is most successful when least obvious. Except for survey research and polling, when logic and flow of a respondent's thought must give way to planned sequence, the skilled oral history interviewer stimulates, invites, or challenges the narrator, artfully dangling sufficient discussion-topic bait so that the narrator wants to talk. A too-overt display of knowledge by the interviewer may put the narrator on the defensive. This is a danger in oral history interviewing, although it can be a wise move in journalistic interviewing.

The oral history interviewer's preparation provides essential but almost concealed groundwork that helps the interview to unroll as though by its own momentum. The interviewer's art and technique are the keys to achieving that kind of movement.

To Stimulate Memory

Memory is the most significant resource for the oral history narrator. Assuming reliance on memory, interviewers need to know what the narrator is most likely to remember, under what circumstances memory can work best, and what kinds of help to offer.

The experiences of two oral history interviewers working nearly two decades apart in different fields support these concepts. First, the narrators seemed relatively unable or unwilling to discuss specifics such as legislative bills or scientific experiments, and tended not to remember them. They responded much more fluently to queries about events in their personal lives. Second, the duration and number of sessions affected both the kinds of questions asked and the quality of the answers.

Thomas S. Kuhn, reporting in 1964 on a project dealing with pioneers in quantum physics, recalled that

With a few very important exceptions our subjects [narrators] displayed only occasional and scattered recollections about the development of their own theoretical and experimental work. . . .
The same men, however, whose memories stuttered when asked to recapitulate the origin, development, or reception of a scientific concept or experiment, were often able to talk with fluency in recreating their home, school, and university lives.[66]

Unwillingness or inability to recall important professional activities was repeated in a different field in 1982 when Sarah Sharp conducted a series of short (two-session) oral history interviews on California state government. She selected narrators to reflect differing perspectives on issues with which they had been closely involved. She noted that they tended to be unresponsive to questions concerning specific items of legislation, which at one time had claimed their most urgent attention.

Subsequently, an interviewers' seminar concluded that specific questions often do not evoke as good answers as less-focused non-directive questions. Further, the combination of directed queries and short sessions tended to change the interviewer's technique from that of classic oral history to something resembling that used for survey research. In addition, longer oral history memoir interviews were more likely than the limited sessions to permit the narrator to become "a companion in research." Finally, the difficulty of establishing rapport in a brief series of short interviews can well mean that narrators are less responsive.[67]

We turn now to the question of rapport as developed in free-wheeling oral history memoir interviews with individual narrators.

Establishing Rapport

The development of some level of rapport—i.e., an harmonious and sympathetic relationship—linking interviewer and narrator, is valuable in any kind of interview, but is essential for oral history.

The narrator's prime resource is memory. If memories are to be evoked, the interviewer must concentrate on the narrator's remarks, expressions, pauses, and stay in tune with the flow of the story. Some interviewers try to aid concentration by visualizing the account as it is being told. Interviewers have remarked that when they lose their own concentration, the narrator will frequently falter, stop, or otherwise signal a break of the narrative thread. For the narrator to tap memory and bring forth even more than might have been expected, the interviewer needs to foster this mysterious process by earned trust, careful preparation, concentration, and genuine interest and delight in the unfolding story. The better the rapport, the fuller and freer the narrator's account is likely to be. At times, an interviewer's success in reducing a narrator's anxiety can help open doors to recollections that may have disappeared from conscious awareness many years earlier.

The deliberate building of rapport gives the oral history interviewer an advantage that not all kinds of interviewers enjoy, i.e., permission to develop a liking for and understanding of the narrator, without fear of being coopted or losing professional distance. Such associational friendships can cross boundaries of political sympathies, age, education, experience, and developed tastes. Openness, shared knowledge, and trust can form bonds between persons who are otherwise unlikely to appreciate or even communicate with each other.[68]

Oral history interviewers' techniques vary. Some rely on the narrators' free associations to bring out significant material. Items on the outline can thus be ticked off as they are covered, and missing items in a sequence marked for attention at another session. Others may exercise more direction, bringing a narrator back to a specific sequence of events or time, and suggesting that the current discussion be deferred until the right moment. These are idiosyncratic, personal differences in style that each oral history interviewer develops, often by trial and error in actual interviewing.

Cutting across all personal preferences are the interviewer's classic methods of providing support, recognition, interest, encouragement, the right word at the right time, or an appropriate silence. When the interviewer is performing well, and rapport and teamwork are well developed, the interviewer and narrator can become close partners in an enterprise that is mutually rewarding.

In addition to skills, attitudes, and intangibles, oral history interviews require such equipment as pencil and paper, tape recorders, and often transcripts. Technology—to which we now turn—has provided aids that greatly facilitate the practice of oral history.

Transcending Technology

Note-taking and tape-recording both characterize the oral history interview, as they do other interview styles. The tape recorder, now usually a cassette in preference to the older and bulkier reel-to-reel machine, is the primary instrument used in capturing interview questions and answers. As the tape runs, the interviewer usually keeps notes to spell difficult words or names and to provide other aids for the transcriber. In tape transcribing, typists normally use foot pedals and ear phones, typing double-spaced transcripts that are later reviewed by the narrators. One hour of a taped interview usually takes about six hours to transcribe.

Before tapes are delivered to a transcriber, however, the interviewer's job is to devote roughly 98 percent of attention to the narrator's story—listening, responding, questioning. The other 2 percent is used to assure that the tape recorder's wheels are turning, the machine is set to record, and that the tape supply has not run out. Cautious interviewers test each side of a tape before proceeding, to be certain that the interview is being recorded and that the microphone is picking up enough sound. Perhaps because the technology is now more familiar and less threatening than it once was, "mike fright" seems now virtually to have disappeared. Interviewers working in the early 60s remember placing a stand-up mike on the table, and then casually tossing a chiffon scarf over it. While the idea was to conceal the mike, it was hard for a nervous narrator to ignore the scarf-covered lump. Newer multidirectional microphones, lavaliere mikes, or horizontal mikes seem far less intrusive, and are apparently easily accepted by the narrators and soon forgotten.

The interviewer's discipline and capacity for listening in a concentrated way may be more significant in the oral history interview than in some others we have examined, although they are also integral to the success of any type of interview. In oral history, the interviewer listens not only to evoke needed information, but also to help the narrator explore and decide on what he or she wants and needs to say. Interviewers thus tend to develop their own aids and reminders: one is the "movie" an interviewer may see with the mind's eye. Narrators relating their stories also appear to be seeing again the episodes and persons they recall. The interviewer can keep on track by attempting to see the same scene as nearly as possible. The questions that follow tend to grow out of the shared experience in a natural sequence.

The Value of Silence

In addition to asking the right questions at appropriate times, an oral history interviewer also needs to understand the value of the pause, of silence, even though the tape is spinning. An interview consists of talk, but it is not the kind of social occasion in which silence may bring unease that needs to be dispelled with small talk. Silence in an oral history interview is not an embarrassment; it may in fact be a necessity, allowing a narrator to reflect, remember, and order thoughts before resuming the spoken part of the interview.

Silence can also be the right choice for an interviewer who may be tempted to volunteer personal information. When the narrator says, for example, "I was elected to Phi Beta Kappa in my junior year," the interviewer may feel the urge to say, "Were you? So was I," with the comforting thought that this community of experience may contribute to rapport. But does it? Is the interviewer enjoying a bit of personal gratification that intrudes on the narrator's story? Probably a smile and a silent nod would be better.[69]

The Ripple Effect

In their conduct and use of interviews historians also confront questions of technique, as well as ethics, effectiveness of communication, control and flexibility, reliability and accuracy—problems that relate to many aspects of research. As ambiguities surrounding interviews are reduced, the results may prove useful in a variety of research procedures.

As an example, oral history interviewing and its methods can provide optional techniques for other professionals, such as historians. Ronald Grele has observed that

the issues raised in oral history automatically become issues in the practice and use of history. As Saul Benison notes . . . "It may be that one of the ultimate values of oral history is that it is a magnificent way of training a young historian to do history."[70]

While recognizing the problems a historian faces as an interviewer, transcriber, and analyst of interviews, there is also applause for historians studying recent history who have "tape recorders in their brief cases and cassettes among their note cards." They have discovered the rich resources of information that ordinary people can provide.

CONCLUSION

Interviewing techniques tend to be style-specific: each interview type calls for a particular cluster of techniques. The well-prepared interviewer who understands the topic and has selected the appropriate narrator and interview type increases the chance to produce effective interviews. The absence of any one of these elements—specificity and understanding, preparation and responsiveness—signals erosion of interview quality. Despite differences among interview types and techniques, however, we note some common threads: the need for effective listening, establishment of rapport (which may simply be "agreeing to disagree"), and clarity about who wants what and how it is to be obtained.

If researchers are going to use interviews, evaluation is the first step. Researchers must find ways to judge the accuracy, completeness, and reliability of the interview material. Knowing the techniques appropriate for each kind of interview gives insight into whose interests are served and how. The researcher needs to be aware of the games the politico-narrarator can play with the journalistic interviewer, and vice-versa; how sampling, wording, and tallying can affect the statistical reliability of the survey or poll; or how the oral history narrator may at times substitute a personal choice of topic and override the plans and preferences of the interviewer. Further, the "question not asked" may reflect any of several decisions: that of the journalist as interviewer, of the editor who shapes the final version, or the choice of the oral history narrator whose blue pencil can delete questions and answers alike.

Finally, understanding the techniques involved, the researcher knows that the narrator's words will be presented directly as spoken and approved in oral history interviews, awaiting only transcription, deposit in a research library or historical society collection, and official release. In contrast, interviews in the journalistic, survey research and polling, and scholarly research styles pass through another level of scrutiny and possible revision by the editor/publisher on the way toward publication.

The role of the editor/publisher is also that of a gatekeeper who determines whether the interview will be discarded or printed sooner or later, and finally in what form. Such authority carries major responsibilities. The next chapter focuses on editorial concerns about interviews, and the ways individual editors and publishers handle them.

V

Editor and Publisher:
Authority, Responsibility,
Scrutiny

INTRODUCTION

The editor makes important choices at two crucial points: before the interviews begin and after they end. In the journalistic interview, the editor often selects the interviewer, the narrator, the topic, and the emphasis. In all interview styles except oral history—designed not for impending publication but for future research—the editor determines when, how, or if the material will be published. Even the researcher who assigns interviews to him- or herself or to specified helpers and uses the outcome for a particular project cannot avoid dealing with an editor somewhere along the path to publication. Although not physically present during interviews, the editor also exerts pressure implicitly throughout their progress. (See Chapter I for definitions of "editor" and "publisher." Unless stated otherwise, the term editor here extends to both roles in setting larger policies concerning interviews. The editor, however, does the hands-on implementation.)

The editor's skill is tested through dealings with the publisher and an array of interviewers: journalists, columnists, social science researchers, pollsters, and others in various settings. As media decisionmakers, editors juggle technical and ethical claims as well as legal limits and protections, e.g., avoiding libel actions and claiming the shelter of the First Amendment. (This discussion focuses on the editorial side of the press, and does not include the business side, e.g., relationships with advertisers and other financial players. They are important, but are outside the purview of this study.)

Focus on Examples

Scrutiny by the public and media colleagues can temper the editor's power; these critics can refer to professional codes in evaluating performance. The following examples draw some distinctions between the powers of editors and of publishers. In addition, we see how editorial authority can combat errors of fact or interpretation, or alternatively introduce bias. Finally, we note to what extent decisionmakers succeed in upholding standards of quality, how they deal with accuracy and the need for corrections, and how they view the performance of columnists, interviewers, and writers in the field.

CODES, STANDARDS, AND RELATIONSHIPS

Reporters, Editors, and Publishers

Earlier discussions of ethical codes focused on standards for reporters. Bruce Swain has raised the matter of "double standards" for reporters and publishers. Referring to "personal [reporters'] and corporate [publishers'] codes" he suggested that

If codes are effective in bolstering reporters' ethics, should not publishers and editors adhere to the same rules? The codes in Louisville and Des Moines say they should. The Sigma Delta Chi [journalism honorary society] code of ethics pointedly and repeatedly refers to "journalists and their employers." But at many papers that question remains unsettled—usually to the advantage of editors and publishers.[1]

Appropriate codes develop slowly. The American Society of Newspaper Editors (ASNE), for example, has struggled with problems of codes and ethics for more than 50 years. When the ASNE board of directors adopted a "Statement of Principles" on October 23, 1975, that act supplanted their 1922 "Canons of Journalism." The statement's Article IV, "Truth and Accuracy" said in part, "Editorials, analytical articles and commentary should be held to the same standards of accuracy with respect to facts as news reports."[2]

Editors and Publishers

Leonard Silk of the *New York Times,* addressing a class of business school graduates at the University of California, Berkeley, differentiated between the views of editors and those of publishers. He said on occasion editors must oppose and argue with publishers—sometimes on matters of principle—to "save their souls." He added that business employees and executives also owed loyalty to employers, but not at the price of their own integrity.[3]

Silk's comments serve as a reminder that editors' and publishers' views are not always compatible. Further, the editor's position can be ambiguous, with a foot in both camps, sometimes being criticized by the journalist-interviewer for acting as the publisher's surrogate, and yet at other times fighting to oppose the publisher's directives.

Editors and Columnists

When the editor holds reporter/interviewers to standards of accuracy in interviews, presumably the same standards would apply to the columnist/interviewers, as the ASNE recommends. This is usually true, but not always.

New York News columnist Michael Daly wrote about a British soldier named "Christopher Spell," identified him and his barracks, and included conversations among members of his patrol. Daly "made it appear that [he] . . . had been on the scene with the patrol before, during and after" a shooting incident in which he reported that Spell fired "live" bullets that wounded a 15-year-old Belfast boy.[4]

In a point-by-point rebuttal, the *London Daily Mail* offered evidence that there was no soldier named Christopher Spell. Further, no reporters were present in an area where a boy had been wounded in an incident reported by the British army, and the patrol involved had not come from the barracks Daly had identified. Daly resigned after saying that he stood by his story, but could not prove it.

When questioned about the column, *News* editor Michael O'Neill acknowledged Daly's use of "misleading journalistic techniques," but indicated that in his paper columnists and reporters are not held to the same standards.

We give columnists a great deal of leeway to express their personal opinions . . . to assure the freest possible flow of ideas . . . . We therefore do not subject columnists to the same rigorous demands of objectivity and factual checking that we apply to news coverage. But . . . we cannot condone the use of techniques that imply that some things are fact when they are not.[5]

Verifying facts does not, however, necessarily impede the free flow of ideas: it might act as a stimulus. Further, the editor's fine discrimination between a reporter's interview and that of a columnist would probably be lost on researchers and other readers concerned with accuracy and reliability.

In one of his well-written articles on journalistic ethics and the ways of editors, David Shaw of the *Los Angeles Times* differentiated between a "writers' newspaper" and an "editors' newspaper," and the level of editorial responsibility involved. In the latter, including the *Wall Street Journal* and the *New York Times*, several editors work on most major stories.

That means these editors are likely to catch more mistakes before publication than at such "writers' newspapers" as the *Washington Post* or *Los Angeles Times*, where writers have traditionally been given more latitude, where heavy editing is generally limited to

the most important major stories and where multiple layers of editors are far less common.[6]
While editors catch pre-publication mistakes, Shaw noted that more errors are discovered after publication because "at an 'editors' newspaper' the editors tend . . . to assume more responsibility for the final product than do their colleagues at a 'writers' newspaper.'"[7]

Even good writers have a hard time catching their own mistakes; therefore the editors' function is critical, particularly because one error caught before publication is worth a flock discovered afterwards.

At the *New York Times* editors and a writer reacted angrily when they found a story with both a misleading headline and editing errors. A. M. Rosenthal, *Times* executive editor, noticed that a headline was wrong, and found two other editors and the writer upset as well. The writer was annoyed because his story "carried a headline that misrepresented what he had written" and had been "edited so that two important paragraphs were missing."[8]

In reaction, Rosenthal established a column called "Editors' Note," where "the *Times* would try to rectify or amplify what its editors considered to be 'significant lapses of fairness, balance or perspective' in the paper." In this instance, the new column did two things: explained what had gone wrong with the headline, and also stated, "in editing to fit available space, two balancing paragraphs reflecting publishers' point of view were omitted. They are printed today on page 15."[9]

Editors and a Special-Case Community

At times journalism requires exceptional promises to be made and kept. A good example is the special agreement between an editor and black ghetto residents in St. Louis regarding access to newspaper columns, provision of a byline, and authority to check and review material. After trying unsuccessfully to gain access to news columns for stories important to them, the ghetto residents met with the newspaper's executive editor to discuss their complaints.

The editor suggested the following solution: "prospective contributors could . . . tell their stories to a reporter, or tape them and a reporter could write them up. . . . " When asked "Could a black person review the article before it was printed?" the editor said that subjects were never allowed to approve articles. He said, however, "a ghetto resident could approve an article . . . under his byline," and gave the further assurance that any article the editor accepted would be published.

Thus by special negotiation the editor sought to make certain that the stories of ghetto residents would be told straight, and would be published— with the assumption that he would not reject them arbitrarily. This agreement gave a level of access that is not available to the general public. It permitted the residents to make use of a byline as an alternative to a journalistic interview, and gave the narrators shared control over the material they contributed.[10]

Ink Media Competing with Electronic Media

The *Columbia Journalism Review,* in a discussion of the Janet Cooke story (below), suggested another point of slippage if editors allow reporters license when newspapers compete with TV for public attention. In such cases, reporters may "reconstruct dialogue and construct supposedly real-life dramas in which the protagonists are unidentified, or are composites of real people, like characters in a novel." The *Review* article called such "journalistic hype" a "debilitating virus," and suggested that "the public's skepticism about what it reads in the newspapers should provide a powerful motive for reform."[11]

Not all editors permit, and not all reporters choose to use, such license. They find ways to protect anonymity where it is actually needed. Fox Butterfield, reporting on interviews recently conducted in China, explained his method of operation:

> As a police state, China poses special problems for a journalist. Many of the most significant insights I gained, or the most poignant anecdotes I heard, came from people I cannot name or portray in detail because of . . . reprisals. . . . Wherever possible, I have identified the people I knew, and wherever a full three-syllable Chinese name appears, like that of the sculptor Wang Keping, it is the name of the actual person.[12]

Where he needed to protect identities, Butterfield used anonymity or invented first or last names. For some, he altered minor details of their lives, such as location or occupation. He added, "but all their comments and quotations are genuine, and none of the characters are composites."[13]

Publishers and Editors

Editors, in turn, may feel selective pressure from publishers. Diana Tillinghast, discussing the publisher's influence on the editorial desk, reported findings from a study of campaign coverage that included California and Pennsylvania. She observed,

> We found no evidence to support the so-called conspiracy theories, i.e., that the personal foibles or biases of publishers affect news judgement on national campaign news. . . .
>
> I want to stress, however, that we are only talking about *national* political news. Local news may be slanted.[14] [emphasis in original]

She found some evidence of manipulation of local government and political news, but this was limited to "the city desk and didn't interfere with the news editor's selection of national political news."[15]

If this pattern is followed, the editor could expect a relatively free hand with interviews concerning national candidates and issues, but might have to accommodate the publisher's views concerning interviews on local political affairs.

SHARING BLAME AND TAKING RESPONSIBILITY

Regardless of a publisher's influence, the editor does wield power—to make assignments, to delete or alter interview material, to shape headlines in a published account, and finally to act as gatekeeper. This preeminent power and visibility also make the editor a fair target for resentment and blame by an interviewer if apparently arbitrary changes occur in a byline article. The interviewer or writer may feel as "misquoted" as a narrator does in an unsatisfactory interview. Equally, the interviewer who feels unprepared may be frustrated by the editorial deadlines that squeeze out time for research. Even more serious is the journalist's complaint, "I want to write the real story, but my editor wants conflict, action, violence."

Getting the Story

When editors put pressure on reporters to produce prize-winning stories and quality control fails, the consequences can backfire. Some observers saw pressure as contributing to Janet Cooke's fabrication, or composite story, about an 8-year-old heroin addict, a boy who did not exist. The story won a Pulitzer Prize, but lost it when executive editor Benjamin Bradlee of the *Washington Post* discovered the hoax and wired the Pulitzer Prize Foundation that "Miss Cooke was declining the prize . . . and resigning . . . . " "Janet Cooke is a talented writer," *Washington Post* publisher Donald Graham said, "That's part of the tragedy. She didn't have to do this."[16]

Bill Green, the *Post*'s ombudsman, noted that the paper's quality control had failed, since no editor had required the writer to reveal her sources to an editor.[17] Thus the editors' performance was also questioned and assigned a share of criticism.

Ironically, Teresa Carpenter of the *Village Voice*, the substitute winner, won citations for three stories including one on the killing of politician Allard Lowenstein. The National News Council, however, called the story on Lowenstein "unfair and reckless," after his brother and James Wechsler, columnist for the *New York Post*, filed a complaint with the council. Criticism centered on Carpenter's suggestion that "Lowenstein made homosexual advances to friends in the civil rights movement," and further on her use of "too many unnamed sources . . . [that] misled readers into believing that Carpenter had interviewed Sweeney [the man charged with Lowenstein's murder]."[18]

The *Voice* reportedly refused to cooperate in the council's investigation, citing in a letter its "unwillingness to 'encourage censure from a self-appointed group.'" The newspaper thus avoided dealing with the substance or merits of the complaint, unlike the *Post's* policy of open self-criticism and acceptance of editorial responsibility.

Page One Fever vs. Protecting the Unwary

The journalistic interviewer who weighs the claims of the narrator and of the editor may well tip the balance to favor the editor. When Bruce M.

Swain, author of *Reporters' Ethics,* asked practicing journalists about ethical behavior, reporter Donald C. Drake responded with an example of speech coverage—rather than an interview—involving Hubert H. Humphrey. Drake said his story hardly mentioned the substance of the speech but reported that a rotten egg was thrown at the speaker. Drake later commented ruefully:

> I wrote the story that way because I knew, without asking, that that's what the [editor's] desk would want, and I wanted good play for the story. . . . In doing so I became a hack, a whore, not only to my profession, but to my paper. . . . [19]

Swain noted that "Even greater detriment to truth can occur when one of those Pavlovian responses, the old-fashioned scoop instinct, is combined with the good play virus." The "scoop," the story no one else has yet, and "good play," or prominent position in the paper—preferably above the fold and on page 1 or near it—make a tempting combination for a reporter. As Swain suggested, the interviewer-reporter infected with the virus may focus on the flashy and sensational and overlook the need for accuracy, balance, judgment, and a decent regard for the interests of the narrator and the reader.

On the other hand, journalistic interviewers often consciously avoid sensationalism. Several responses by interviewers struck a more ethical balance as they reported such devices as the call-back to check facts or quotes. In response to Swain's queries, Carol Lacey recognized the possibility of narrators' fear and mistrust of the media, and dealt with it, for example by calling back to check facts on technical, medical, or scientific stories.[20] Swain also cited the practice of "protecting the unwary." Such practices would make sure the narrator understands what the interviewer is doing, and avoids the use of unnecessarily destructive quotes by the unwary or unsophisticated.

Wire Services and Corrections

Press associations and wire services purvey news and features to the media. Their customers are editors, publishers, and writers who in turn serve readers. The editors of those services have specific problems in case of error: to inform their clients so that they can in turn inform the eventual consumers.

The *Los Angeles Times* published an Associated Press story that appeared in two releases, September 4 and 21, 1981. It was presented as a first-person account of a "high-speed, multi-car race . . . at speeds up to 200 mph," written by AP reporter Gloria Ohland. It later proved to contain "misrepresentations, quotations and material lifted from a magazine." Ohland told her Los Angeles editor, Steve Loeper, that her story was a composite. In the interval between the two releases, Loeper had learned about the nature of the story, but made no clarification or explanation to the customers of Associated Press.

When questioned about his failure to inform AP's customers, Loeper was quoted in the *Times* as saying he thought the story was a "representative portrayal" and therefore he had made no changes or explanations in the second release. He acknowledged that this was "a very bad mistake . . . in judgment."[21] Reporter Ohland resigned.

The code of the Associated Press Managing Editors implied general principles that would include correction of error. Such correction by a wire service poses different problems from those of a single newspaper, but those differences are primarily technical rather than ethical. Loeper's comment appears to endorse the need and obligation to get corrections out to the customers.

Editor/Publisher at the Desk
and Interviewer/Writer in the Field

During World War II *Time* magazine provided a classic example of the editor vis-à-vis the interviewer on the scene: publisher Henry Luce and reporter Annalee Jacoby. Luce was a friend and supporter of Chiang Kai-shek; the *Time* reporters in China were moving away from his view as they sought to discover and understand political reality on the scene. Halberstam recounted that

> In the early fall of 1944 she [Annalee Jacoby] interviewed Chiang. It was a mild interview, of mild questions. She sent it off [to *Time* magazine] and both she and [Theodore H.] White were stunned later when it came out *completely rewritten;* worse, *questions that had not been asked and answers that had never been given were printed.* It was more anti-Communist and more upbeat about victory.[22] [emphasis added]

On the other hand, publishers usually check with authors about changes. Mary Ellen Leary noted, for example, that

> The *LA Times* (op-ed page) is meticulous about clarifying and reading the final copy as it is going in, noting changes from the original. . . . it is customary if an author says, "but I wanted that in for such-and-such purpose" to usually accept that and make a cut elsewhere to stay within space.[23]

Editors and publishers of newspapers and news services may tend to operate differently from those of news magazines. Ben H. Bagdikian referred to correspondents' and narrators' "endemic complaints" against news magazines, attributable in part to the complex process by which a correspondent's interview finally reaches print.

> The interview is sent to New York where editors, combining it with perhaps dozens of their interviews and other research, convert it all into a brief narrative designed to be concise and dramatic. In the process they frequently take a single phrase from a sentence of one of the interviews and use that phrase as a useful fragment in the mosaic of the whole story. Yet often, this fragmentary phrase may be the direct opposite of the narrator's meaning.
>
> I once told such an interviewer, so-and-so "made errors in his story, but they are minor and do not negate the validity of his viewpoint." It came out that so-and-so "made errors."[24]

Writers for journals can also find unexpected and unauthorized editorial changes in articles published with their bylines. John Westcott, a graduate student in the Graduate School of Journalism, University of California, Berkeley, had worked as an intern with a local paper and written his master's thesis on Berkeley politics. An article adapted from his thesis was published in the *California Journal* not long before Berkeley's April 1981 municipal election. When he saw it, Westcott wrote a letter to the *Journal* and "To Whom It May Concern" stating that the article as published, contained "glaring inaccuracies," including a new paragraph that was "blatantly false." He said further that the article was "rewritten substantially, without my knowledge or consent."[25]

Asked three years later to comment on the episode, Ed Salzman, former *Journal* editor, later capitol bureau chief for the *Sacramento Bee*, and editor and publisher of *Golden State Report*, recalled that the problem was totally unexpected and was related to the "shelf-life" of journal articles in general. The effort to keep the story fresh and up-to-date caused a staff member to read of Berkeley developments in the daily press. She misinterpreted the news accounts, and incorporated errors in the rewrite, unaware of any difficulty.

Westcott remembered calling the *Journal* prior to publication to ask whether there were questions or problems, and being asked only about differences in two rent control initiatives—a point he had not mentioned in his article. Salzman did not remember the phone calls, and felt that the *Journal's* corrective measures were "more than adequate." They included a boxed "Correction" in the May 1981 issue that noted "an editing error" and quoted "one paragraph that was not factual . . . and should be disregarded."[26] The *Journal* also mailed copies of Westcott's letter to subscribers in envelopes that did not identify the sender. Westcott ascribed the difficulties to "problems of distance and lack of familiarity between editors and writers." Salzman wondered why the writer of this paper was asking about "an unimportant detail in an unimportant story."[27]

Controlling Access: Medical Publication

If Freud had rephrased his famous question about women as "What do editors want?" a chorus of news editors probably would have answered, "To publish the story first." This need to be first points up the urgency of an interviewer's gaining access to the narrator and the story. If the narrator's field is medical research, he or she in turn will seek access to a prestigious publication such as *The New England Journal of Medicine,* that is "generally regarded as America's leading medical journal." A dilemma arose when Franz Ingelfinger was editor of the *Journal* and ruled in 1969 that it would refuse "to publish studies reported elsewhere, including *newspaper articles based on interviews with the researchers.*[28] [emphasis added] The *Journal's* 1969 policy form letter stated that the

> restriction does not apply to abstracts published in connection
> with scientific meetings, or to news reports based *solely* on formal
> and public oral presentations at such meetings, but press confer-

ences at these meetings are discouraged.[29] [emphasis in the original]

In 1981, the current editor, Arnold S. Relman, pointed out that cautioning would-be *Journal* authors against press conferences has led to

the misapprehension that *any* conversation with reporters to clarify what was said at a meeting will disqualify a manuscript. Although the unreviewed and unpublished work presented at scientific meetings is often not a reliable source of information for the public, it is important that reporters who do cover such meetings get their facts straight. The *Journal* does not object if authors help them [presumably with interviews], provided that this does not result in the prior publication of the essential substance of a manuscript submitted to us.[30]

This logic may result in over-cautious interpretations of "essential substance," and place would-be narrators in a state of permanent anxiety. As they see the hazards of overstepping the *Journal's* strictures concerning comments on formal presentations or explaining what was said, the decision may well be to play it safe and keep silent.

Relman also held that news accounts that do not include evidence are "risky sources of information to the public and cannot be very useful to the profession." He added, however, that when the evidence is published, "the popular press can play a very important part in reporting and explaining the new developments to the public."[31]

Other professional journals have taken issue with the rule. Editors of the *Journal of the American Medical Association* charged that as a consequence, "doctors refuse to discuss their work before it is [formally] published, resulting in incomplete and inaccurate reporting of the latest medical developments."[32] Since the authors who are the source of the most complete and accurate information are off-limits for interviews, presumably only the next-best sources would be available. Information-users thus can be shortchanged, and would-be narrators are caught in a tangle of editor vs. editor competition. Finally, if the narrators refuse opportunities for interviews or articles in other publications (including newspapers and other journals), they might still not find a place in the preferred publication, and lose the chance for timely announcement and early discussion of their work.

The Editorial Function in Social Research

Social, biomedical, behavioral science, and technological research impose specialized kinds of responsibility on editors as well as researchers. Editors need to understand that in social research, primary ethical concerns relate to protecting the privacy of persons interviewed and the subjects of experiments, as well as to avoidance of possible injury to them. The Society for Research in Child Development, for example, has adopted a code of ethics with numerous safeguards to protect the child's well-being. It concludes:

Instructors should communicate ethical concerns to their students

and *journal editors should be on guard for ethical transgression.*[33]
[emphasis added]
To evaluate ethics, research methods, substance, and evidence has always
been part of the editor's responsibility. The primary difference appears to be
that now he or she must expect to share criticism when readers find fault with
published research.

Psychologists Bernie Zilbergeld and Michael Evans were quoted as
commenting that the research of William Masters and Virginia Johnson was
"so flawed by methodological errors and slipshod reporting that it fails to
meet customary standards . . . for evaluation research." They also made an
additional point: "Masters and Johnson were not 'totally responsible for all
the problems in their work.'" The two "were not well served by their *editors,
colleagues, and readers who failed to point out errors or ask 'hard questions.'"*
[emphasis added] Zilbergeld and Evans thus found both editorial and peer
review flawed.[34]

While "colleagues and readers" may be an amorphous lot, editors are
easily identified. Zilbergeld and Evans's comments sound harsh, but conscientious editors would probably agree that they should know the kinds of questions to ask researchers, interviewers, and respondents and should also share
responsibility for eliminating errors as far as possible in research and reporting.

CONCLUSION

Editors can seem both remote and demanding when they issue assignments to and expect prize-winning performance from interviewers who struggle with deadlines and competition, ethical imperatives, and slippery narrators. Editors, however, also field their share of criticism, e.g., for allowing
reporters license to enhance dramatic values with "composite persons" and
"reconstructed dialogue." If communication fails between editors and columnists, editorial misjudgments and errors can follow, with possible legal
difficulties and/or charges of libel.

Further, editors of technical, social, and scientific journals may find
themselves cast as judges of last resort in matters of ethics and the professional competence of researchers, writers, and interviewers. Those who fail to
ask enough of the right questions may allow standards of professional research
to decline by publishing material that is poorly prepared and based on inadequate reporting. To perform at the optimum, the editor needs to be a skilled
interviewer of staff and contributors, as well as an expert listener.

To further complicate matters, tight editorial control over access to publication by groups and individuals can raise issues of fairness, First Amendment rights, and even censorship. Seeking a balance, editors are well advised
to be ready to defend their decisions from the pointed questions of publishers,
readers, and media watchers in general.

Our approach has highlighted problems on selected occasions when even skillful editors suffer lapses. It is equally important to see the ways they recognize errors and seek to maintain excellent performance. Quality control appears in every phase of the process, and at the end editors must decide whether the article should be published, and if so how much of it, and with what sorts of excerpts, deletions, and headlines. Here we confront a major responsibility: determining access to the printed page.

The wit who said, "Freedom of the press is guaranteed to anybody who owns one," also implied the reverse for individuals or groups who depend on public media to circulate their concerns or gain attention for their points of view. As newspapers die or are bought out by competitors, monopoly tends to shrink opportunities for access. When the editor of the only paper in town refuses space for an interview story, there may be little if any alternative for publication.

Finally, the researcher who reads and wishes to use the published interview or byline story evaluates the judgment, skill, and guidance of the editor as well as that of the interviewer. Are quotes attributed to real persons? Are sources named? Does reliable evidence support conclusions? Are the assumptions, ground rules, and error tolerances acknowledged? Have the "hard" editorial questions been asked? If so, editorial authority has been exercised well, and the material can be accepted. On the other hand, there is no way for the reader to know if the editor has been unduly rigid or arbitrary in excluding a potentially valuable interview or story. Since other stories fill the available space like water filling a hole, no evidence remains of what may have been lost.

VI

Whether to Interview: Why and When, Pro and Con

THE BEST PART

The journalist's formula for a good news story—who, what, when, where, why, and how—can also apply to interviews. We have considered those who conduct and use interviews (who); types of interviews (what); and the principles that shape them (how). We now turn to the other three queries: why, when, and where.

Put differently, why, when, and where do interviews become the method of choice? Why should one choose to conduct and use interviews rather than finding other ways to gain information? The questions, however, imply too narrow a choice. The answer is not always either/or, but often both/and, both interviews and other sources. Even when the decision to use and conduct interviews is the right one, interviews are seldom the exclusive alternative. More often they supplement or complement other information sources, helping to verify or being verified as well as supplying new information that may be unavailable elsewhere.

Their characteristics suggest both their strengths and weaknesses. Oral history interviews and written memoirs alike rest on perception and memory. Assertions of "fact" must be checked. A journalistic interview requires background for building a context; a survey or opinion poll calls for interpretation and reference points in a framework of theory or events.

Many researchers see interviewing as the "best part" of a project; they respond to the "larger human sense" that gives interviewing its charm. In fact, book-writing journalists like David Halberstam and David S. Broder, who use hundreds of interviews, seem never to tire of them.[1] While library research, data interpretation, writing, and editing can be rewarding, interviewing remains the runaway favorite, whether it involves a single meeting, or comprises a complex series that may continue for years.[2]

Rewarding though they often are, interviews still should be subjected to a cost-benefit test, whether the cost is tallied in time, effort, and/or dollars. Further, the individual circumstances and conditions of an interview can make pre-judging difficult. Pros and cons enter into each decision, whether to interview or not, to use one interview rather than another, or whether to avoid the form entirely. With what we have learned about interview types and the expectations they raise, we are ready to examine options and make critical choices with some confidence.

Focus on Examples

Here we can observe some of the consequences of choosing an interview type to supply information, and at the same time recognize the significance of the interview's context.

Examples suggest the kinds of conditions that reveal interviews as a good choice: when they extend the reporter's own capacities to dig out information, provide the latest insights, or serve as a vehicle for feedback on public policy. In addition, the interviewer can serve as a catalyst to activate the narrator's memory. Finally, interviews can either work well combined with other sources, or provide the sole source when others are not available.

Interviews can also be the wrong choice for information-gathering, if other methods would be more efficient and cost-effective, or if faulty ethics or poor technique reduce the value of the product. Sometimes interviews are used to substitute for the interviewer's own insights and analysis, and mask a failure to investigate, think, and interpret.

USEFUL PRODUCT AND BENEFICIAL CONSEQUENCE

The right kind of interview, well conducted, can provide a cornucopia of benefits, both in product and process. The product can present information efficiently, encourage the ongoing cooperation of participants, and earn the confidence of users. The process itself can be rewarding and bring the added benefit of mutual respect among the persons involved.

With regard to efficiency, an interview can be a powerful research tool, clear of focus and elegant in operation. Knowing what information is needed, the researcher can evaluate trade-offs, e.g., weighing the controls of survey research and "dry data" against the color and challenge of journalistic interviews, or such alternatives as selective scholarly interviews with their thoughtful assessment and careful interpretation, vs. oral history's statement of an individual's recollections and views.

The second benefit is long-term productivity, a continuing source of information. The interviewer who does a good job can call again on the narrator, who may well become an ally and a source of networking, tips, and further suggestions. The researcher or interviewer who is welcomed back will find more and better material over a longer time than one who exploits the narrator once, and is not trusted in that neighborhood again.

The third benefit is confidence and ability to rely on the product. Reliability does not mean that every word or every interview is "true" and should be accepted without verification. Reliability does mean that each interview carries an invisible label: "Use only as directed."[3] (The researcher who knows how to select the most appropriate interview style can also best evaluate the interviews of others.) Evaluating reliability means remembering, for example, that a journalistic interview is analogous to a tennis match; the interviewer and narrator see each other as contestants, but the interviewer also wears the hat of the line judge, who can call "fault" against the narrator. It means that an oral history interview relates exactly what the narrator chooses to say. Thus oral history offers personal perception and memory that are valuable in themselves, while serving to remind the researcher of the need to check with other sources for verification.

The final consequence of well chosen and well conducted interviews is the cultivation of mutual respect. More diffuse than the other benefits, it is also the most pervasive, touching all participants and users. Respect does not require the interviewer's liking, agreement, or even sympathy; it requires only the recognition that narrators are persons, not objects, data, targets, or victims. If the narrators are outstanding, the interview is not the place to praise them. If they are evil-doers, the interviewer should still quote accurately.

Respect does not require the velvet glove, but does mean treatment according to the rules. Respect is cultivated when the interviewer makes the rules clear to the narrator and follows through, the narrator understands process and choices, the editor avoids distortions or arbitrary alterations in the published account, and finally, when the researcher quotes accurately and interprets thoughtfully.

Interviewing as the Right Choice

Just how useful and important can interviews be? To dramatize the journalist's need, let us imagine that interviews were forbidden. Libraries, reference material, and the journalist's own personal observations would still be usable sources, as would government documents, financial reports of industries, scientific and academic reports. But no expert could be consulted, no politician could oblige with "quotable quotes," no narrator's first-hand experiences could be related. Background consultation, tips and networking, interpretation: all would be absent.

True enough, the reporter's eye-witness presence would add authenticity to reports of city council meetings and congressional debates, but timing and logistical problems would multiply with too many meetings and not enough time to cover them.[4] Short of becoming a voracious reader in the I. F. Stone tradition, the journalist who could not interview would suffer a narrowing of range and find it hard to replace the fresh information and ideas that interviews provide.

At their best, both journalistic and scholarly research interviews, as well as completed oral history interviews, can produce information more readily than other sources, or at times reveal what cannot be found through other means. Lacey Fosburgh noted, for example, that newspaper morgues and files are sources for background and historical information, but lack the "newest of the new" that journalists seek. She also saw the journalistic interview as an essential source of current human issues, "the stuff of life," a necessary component for virtually all journalistic reports.[5]

Further, for an impressionistic view of "public mood or sentiment, or response to an event," the semi-journalistic "man in the street" interview can give a fresh and spontaneous response. The researcher looking for statistically reliable results at a particular time on specific questions would turn to polling or survey research. For telling quotes and individual views developed at some length, the journalistic or scholarly interview would serve best.

The Power of the Question, or Narrator as Sleeping Beauty

Where interviews are the best choice, the well-prepared interviewer can also serve as catalyst, creating the chemistry that helps a narrator retrieve information or insights that may be hidden away in memory.

Two kinds of problems of memory and communication are illustrated by (1) a contemporary American political figure, Robert S. Strauss, and (2) a historically significant English inventor, Charles Babbage. Two intelligent and sympathetic interviewers, Elizabeth Drew and Ada, Countess of Lovelace, helped their respective narrators resolve their problems.

In the first example, Drew interviewed Strauss, prominent in national Democratic Party politics. She asked how he "keeps in his head all the political data he draws upon." He replied

I don't know what I know. I have a pretty good encyclopedia of
America, but I couldn't recite it. . . . If you ask me to write what I
know, I could maybe fill a page. But if you ask me a hundred
questions, I could tell you the answers.[6]

Strauss's reply combined the importance of questions to stimulate memory with the fact that he, like many others, found it easier to talk than to write. With rapport between interviewer and narrator, the answers could flow with ease.

The Babbage example shows how a focused interviewer can draw information from a narrator who may not be sure what is needed to express his ideas clearly. The brilliant 19th century English mathematician had invented the calculator and developed the concept of the computer long before the technology existed to make it workable. He found difficulties in explaining his ideas for the "analytical engine." The Countess, "an exceptional mathematician," understood him well enough to write: "The Analytical Engine weaves algebraical patterns just as the Jacquard loom weaves flowers and leaves."

Wishing to learn more, she met Babbage, and "set out to study his designs for the analytical engine in depth, *filling in any blank spots by pulling them out of his head in conversation.*"[7] [emphasis added]

Both interviewers succeeded in helping the narrators remember and communicate. Strauss did not know all that he knew, and by himself Babbage could not see what he had omitted in explaining his visionary ideas.

Interviews as Feedback

Interviews can help solve another problem: timeliness. Prompt response and feedback often are essential if public policies are not to be overtaken by events.

With respect to economic policies and decisions, Eli Ginsberg noted that

Reality changes more rapidly than analysis can master it. . . . Given this obstacle, we dare not use inadequate knowledge as an excuse for nonintervention. . . . [W]e . . . must . . . pursue our common goals with a flexibility that enables us to make adjustments as feedback information becomes available and as our understanding . . . is enlarged.[8]

To Circumvent a "Banning Order"

If unchallenged, politically induced silence can distort current history and quiet the voices of opposition, but a variety of devices, including tape-recorded interviews, can permit such voices to be heard. Under a "banning order" from South Africa's government, Winnie Mandela was forbidden to engage in a list of political educational activities "or to take any part whatever in preparing any kind of publication."[9] As the wife of Nelson Mandela, imprisoned head of the African National Congress, and a leader in her own right, she was forbidden to address a meeting, much less be involved in preparing a book. Nevertheless, the book, *Part of My Soul Went With Him* was published. Her contribution to the book occurred when she and West German journalist Anne Benjamin met for several tape-recorded interviews beginning in 1983, and defied the banning order.

Benjamin then edited the interview material plus personal letters and anecdotes from Mandela's friends, as well as additional historical material by Mary Benson, a South African writer. Book reviewer Dan Bellm noted that "through the gracious help of friends [Winnie Mandela] . . . is able to speak to us directly in a clear voice—generous and vulnerable, but also tough." The words of other writers and contributors were important elements in the book, but those of Mandela herself, spoken in her own voice, were the inspiration and central impulse for the publication.

Silence and Absence

Sometimes absence rather than presence of expected documents stirs the writer's imagination. When historian T. Harry Williams considered writing a biography of the late Huey P. Long, he learned that no one else was planning such a work, "apparently because no significant collection of Long manuscripts was known to exist." He therefore determined to "use the technique of oral history as basic research . . . [10] Williams's brilliant use of interviews contributed to his winning the Pulitzer Prize, the National Book Award, and the Carey Thomas Award for Distinguished Publishing—all honoring his biography, *Huey Long*. The quality of the information is matched by that of the writing. The book remains a delight to read years after Long's death in 1935 and the book's publication in 1969.

Williams's eight-page "Bibliographical Essay" is noteworthy for two reasons. He began with a discussion of oral history, an explanation of the way he and his researchers interviewed the 295 listed individuals, and how he used excerpts from other oral histories from the Columbia University Oral History Project to round out his information. He also listed additional sources: manuscripts, national and state government documents, newspapers and magazines, articles in periodicals and newspapers, books, dissertations, and theses. This listing exemplified the variety of combinations that enriched his prodigious research, and overcame the handicap presented both by Long's death decades earlier, and by the absence of Long manuscripts.

A type of oral history interviewing also came to the rescue more recently in the People's Republic of China. There was a serious lack of written information with respect to cultural matters after the close of the Cultural Revolution. Where war, revolution, and associated events had made other documentation unavailable, the oral history style of interview rescued memories.

When Professor Cyril Birch went to China in January 1980 to seek information on the state of writing and the theater, he found old writers newly returned from the rustication imposed during the Cultural Revolution. They were surrounded by younger staff members and researchers eager to hear and to preserve the elders' thoughts, experiences, and memories. During their years of displacement, the older artists had not been able to write or keep records.[11] To capture living fragments and memories of the cultural past, the young staff members used a kind of oral history interview as an important method of filling the gaps of those silent years.

For Chinese in a different time and context, interviews have also proved valuable in supplementing fragmentary and ephemeral writings in somewhat the way oral histories do. The contemporary book *Island* provides an example of both the techniques for such supplements and the motive for capturing ethnic, folkloric, or community memories that sustain a collective history.

The story of *Island* as a book began with writings in Chinese characters—mostly poetry—inscribed on the walls of the former immigration and detention center at Angel Island in San Francisco Bay. The poems were discovered by a park ranger 30 years after the center's closing; they had been written by Chinese immigrants waiting and hoping to enter the United States. The unused center was slated for demolition, but was finally saved after a dramatic community effort. Three young descendants of former Angel Island detainees determined to translate the poems and provide further historical documentation for the experiences that had sparked the poems. They located and interviewed 39 persons, including 32 who had been held in the detention station.

The interviewers asked the immigrants why they had left home—mostly in and near Canton—to come to *Gam Saan*, "the Golden Mountain" or San Francisco; to describe the time of waiting on the island; and to talk about their experiences. The authors saw the results, with translations of the poems, as giving both "a fairly consistent and accurate picture" of daily life in detention, and the profound emotions expressed in the allusive poetry.

The authors acknowledged that among other problems, those of communication due to cultural and language differences may have caused some of the misunderstandings between immigrants and officials. The interviews, combined with the poems, served to transcend the other difficulties and tell the stories with accuracy and clarity.[12]

Apparently the interviews were reworked into statements varying in length from a few lines to several columns of type. The text did not include the questions, and did not indicate whether material was to be deposited at a research facility. In addition, the narrators received assurances of anonymity. For these reasons, these interviews would not be styled oral histories, although the personal memories are vivid, poignant, and powerful.[13]

In sum, *Island* demonstrated understanding of the value of interviews in capturing memories and explaining the impulses that gave rise to the poems. Further, the authors showed meticulous regard for accuracy, stating their motives and methods at each step, and succeeded in capturing rare historical material, both poems and memories, that otherwise would soon disappear.[14]

Oral history interviews were pronounced "indispensable" by Geoffrey Wigoder of the Hebrew University of Jerusalem. He gave three examples of "areas of modern Jewish history for which there is little or no written documentation." They included the Holocaust, the experience of Jews in Arab lands, and the experience of Jews in the USSR. First,

> The Jews in the ghettos, the resistance, and the camps did not, for the most part, have the opportunity to keep written records. After the war [World War II], the main documentation available for this era was from the German side. . . .

Second, the Jews in Arab lands formed communities that have now largely disappeared, and "the Jews who left were unable to bring out archives and documents." Third, with respect to Jews inside the Soviet Union, "Knowledge was based on . . . scraps of information. . . . Now, with the immigration from the USSR, it is possible to piece together a vivid picture of their way of life, struggle to survive and fight to emigrate . . . "[15]

Oral Tradition or Oral History: Some Distinctions

The foregoing examples show oral history interviews providing vital and perhaps the only records for whole communities of people whose history would otherwise be lost. How does this use compare with the older practices of oral tradition—the memorization and recital of oral information and history by designated wise persons in semiliterate and preliterate societies?

There are both similarities and differences, but the writer believes that the differences are greater. Both rely on oral statements, and use memory to record information and convey a record either to the memories of others or to a tape or printed page. The differences, however, are more revealing both as to the content of the narrative, and the role of a questioner or interviewer.

Some oral history narrators may quote oral tradition as part of their own recollections, repeating concepts that they have accepted and that have shaped their understanding. But whereas the oral tradition tends to be presented as a unified, accepted, and even revered version, oral history reflects each individual's own perception and experience, regardless of agreement or disagreement with an "official" version or with the perceptions of others. Variety is a hallmark of oral history; different narrators' versions of the same events can give perspective, and the personal perspectives add value. They may be in part mutually supportive, but total agreement is not necessary or may not even be desirable.

Oral tradition may be carried on by numerous elders, but in some practices, as that of the griot described below, the speaker is a designated individual (or more than one), who has been trained to recall and recite precisely those agreed-upon myths and reports of actual events that the collective wisdom has accepted as the "official" version of the group's history and culture.

Alex Haley recounted in *Roots* what he learned about African *griots,* the keepers of oral tradition.

A senior *griot* would be a man usually in his late sixties or early seventies; below him would be progressively younger *griots*—and apprenticing boys, so a boy would be exposed to those *griots'* particular line of narrative for forty or fifty years before he could qualify as a senior *griot,* who told on special occasions the centuries-old histories of villages, of clans, of families, of great heroes.[16]

Haley learned of a living *griot* Kebba Kanji Fofana, who knew about his own clan, and went to Africa to meet him.

The old man sat down, facing me. . . . Then he began to recite for me the ancestral history of the Kinte clan, as it had been passed along orally down across centuries from the forefathers' time. It was not merely conversational, but more as if a scroll were being read.[17]

Haley's image of the scroll is apt; the griot was "reading" the scroll of his own prodigious memory trained for that purpose. Inscribed on the griot's scroll was precisely what had been inscribed on that of his teacher, an earlier griot, and so on back to the community's earliest memories and recognition that they should be preserved.

At times an oral history memoirist may also "read" from the scroll of his or her own memory, but the inscription was placed there by the narrator's own experiences and perceptions, and not by the official instruction of a predecessor. It bears the weight of a personal existence, and is at the opposite pole from a preliterate, agreed-upon historical memory that bears responsibility for preserving tribal or community identity.

Presumably the basic accounts in an oral tradition may vary over time as the result of political or other pressures. But at any one time, the story remains the same regardless of questions or the way questions are phrased. As readers and writers whose literacy has made feats of memory less important, we are delighted and astonished at the factual accuracy that seems possible in oral tradition. Haley heard the griot recite events and pinpoint dates in the history of his ancestral African village that meshed exactly with those he had found in his research in official written records a continent away.

Thinking of the griot's great store of knowledge and memory, Haley observed, "today it is rightly said that when a griot dies, it is as if a library has burned to the ground."[18]

Believing in such oral tradition, the amateur archaeologist Heinrich Schliemann (1822-1890) had accepted at face value the visionary legends and tales sung by Homer (as eventually written down and published by others). Guided by the text of Homer's *Iliad*, Schliemann and his workers dug in the village of the Hissarlik on the Asian side of northwestern Turkey until they found the location of the lost city of Troy. In fact they dug past it. Schliemann's heir, Wilhelm Dorpfeld, later found "Homer's Troy to be the sixth level up from the bottom which Schliemann had cut through in his haste."[19] Homer's tale had guided the archaeologists to the right spot.

Such feats of disciplined collective memory are the glories of oral tradition. They are a unique kind of narrative, not to be confused with the oral histories of different eras and different cultures.

PROS AND CONS OF INTERVIEWS

Along with the numerous benefits they can convey, interviews can also present two dangers to plague interviewers and researchers. The first danger, that of choosing the wrong instrument, arises where interviews clearly are not an effective research method and probably should not be used. The second danger, using the right instrument in the wrong way, arises with attempts to make interviews alone provide the basis for interpretation and analysis when they are inadequate to do so without other supporting evidence.

Before sharpening the pencil or testing the cassette tapes, the would-be interviewer needs to make certain determinations. First, he or she should evaluate costs and benefits of the contemplated interview, including whether the time is appropriate and whether the costs and effort will pay off. Next comes the question of whether the information can possibly be found more cheaply and efficiently from other sources, e.g., through a literature survey, or elicited by mailed questionnaires. It may be easier to deal logically with such factual evaluations than with the more emotional aspect: interviews can be fun and exciting, and it is a rare interviewer who can turn away from such promise without a wrench of disappointment.

Interview Costs and Benefits

The interviewer may, for example, need to choose between mailed questionnaires and personal interviews. Costs and benefits of the two techniques can be charted as in Table 1, "Interviewers'/Researchers' Options: Questionnaires vs. Interviews." Additional choices and considerations could also be included.

Except in the case of survey research, all replies may not be equal. Table 1, for example, can help the interviewer recognize trade-offs, but does not provide answers in the making of critical choices about data collection. Thus recognizing options—whether to interview, as well as when to interview—becomes a conscious and positive part of the research process.

Cost evaluation should take into account several matters related to timing. The first is the time and effort required of the interviewer and the narrator. Inappropriate choices at this point are costly both in dollars and in effectiveness. With respect to positions on a public policy issue, an interview may be of limited value if conducted while the issue is still in the formative stages, and may be more productive when the situation has matured. Similarly, oral history interviews can waste time and effort and fail to obtain maximum information if conducted too early, while the narrator still has major accomplishments ahead. Conversely, of course, oral histories may also come too late, after age and illness have seriously weakened energies and memory.

As a start, it is useful to calculate the time invested in each interview session. Next, to each hour of actual interviewing time, additional hours must be tallied, e.g., for question preparation, field tests, scheduling and rescheduling, missed appointments and finding substitute narrators as needed, tallying and analysis of results if appropriate. With variations according to interview style, 20 sessions do not equal 20 to 30 hours, but can rise to 100 hours and counting.

Additional costs to be considered include monetary outlays for the interviewer's salary, research and preparation, transportation, transcription of tapes, phone calls, and other expenses. Money spent on interviews may preclude opportunities for other research activities, e.g., site visits, personal observation, and literature searches.

Cost analysis and budgeting give rise to a number of questions. Considering a journalistic interview, would library research be a cheaper and more productive way of developing background if the name or insights of the narra-

TABLE 1

Interviewers'/Researchers' Options: Questionnaires vs. Interviews

Consideration	Method/Option	
	Mailed Questionnaires	Interviews
Choice of narrators/respondents	Respondents self-selected from pool. Interviewer has no control over who answers: desired respondent, other household members, casual visitor.	Interviewer chooses narrator.
Response rate	Ranges widely.	Can be close to 90% with use of alternate (substitute) narrators.
Timing of response	Variable, some answer within the time limit, others lag. Follow-up usually needed.	Narrator controls meeting time; delay may mean denial. Once interview is obtained, interviewer accomplishes goal, controls timing of process.
Quality of response	Variable, ranges from full response, few or many omissions, to no response. Rejection may offer no second chance for questions. Narrator may misunderstand instructions.	Narrator may answer fully, selectively, or not at all. Adept interviewer has opportunity to gain answers by varied or oblique approach; chance for interaction; ability to minimize misinterpretations.
Tasks and time demands on interviewer	Compile lists of names and addresses; test, prepare, and mail questionnaires; monitor and tally returns; follow-up laggards; write up. No travel time.	Select narrators; make appointments; plan and conduct interviews; analyze and write up. Travel and waiting time.
Monetary costs	Prepare and duplicate questionnaires; mailing costs; follow-up costs of phoning and/or letters.	Travel costs; appointment and follow-up phone calls. Materials minor in cost. Minimal or no postage.
Comparability	Easy to compare, classify, and tally answers.	May be harder to compare, but answers may be richer.

Note: A pro-and-con tally like this may be useful for interviewer's decisions primarily when other considerations are relatively equal, i.e., the same number of narrators would be sought in either case; questions could be posed in relatively simple form so that individual and elaborate explanations would not be needed. This table relates primarily to information gathering. Hypothesis testing for scientific inquiry may require other considerations.

tor contribute little or nothing to the salience of the story? For survey research and polling as well as scholarly research interviews, are the materials obtained likely to be significant enough to justify the costs and effort? Would selective correspondence be more productive? Further, is interview time to be used for matters that the narrator has already covered in published writings? These and similar questions can help determine whether the interview is or is not likely to serve.

Hazards: Interviews by Others

When others do the interviewing, the researcher should be aware of possible hazards, i.e., a questioner's preparation may be faulty; a narrator's dubious or unevaluated information may have been accepted too readily; opportunities to ask valuable new spur-of-the-moment questions may have been missed; or other available sources may not have been checked to provide verification. (A researcher doing his/her own interviewing could also fall into the same traps, but presumably would be forewarned to avoid them.)

If an interviewer assigned to work on a major political issue lacks enough time, money, and background to conduct an effective session, the resulting short-cuts may produce superficialities, vagueness, and ambiguity as well as the use of jargon that can mask ignorance. Ill-prepared interviewers can cause difficulties in every style of interviewing. Much of the following discussion, however, focuses on journalistic interviewers because they are the most visible and familiar, though by no means the only ones that come to grief or cause it.

Professional journalists have recognized the problems of inadequate preparation and lack of special background. Thus Richard Reeves has deplored "the superficiality endemic to generalist journalism." While acknowledging that some reporters have expert knowledge in economics, foreign policy, or agriculture, Reeves cautioned, "those that do are almost always working for the largest news organizations in the country." By implication, he excluded most of the nation's other journalist-generalists. Reeves added, "It pains me to say this, but the people who cover politics generally don't know a damn thing about economics or foreign policy."[20]

The State of Economics Reporting

Economics reporting by journalists provides a rich source of complaints, and often demonstrates how lack of expertise can reduce the value of interviews. Chris Welles, director of the Walter Bagehot Fellowship Program in Economics and Business Journalism at Columbia University, offered some criticisms of economics reporting. He cited journalists' lack of background and preparation, and their apparent unwillingness or inability to gather evidence and scrutinize its implications. Further, he saw reporters failing to provide context for their stories or to offer informed criticism of economic events and evaluate discussions.[21]

Welles's message to interviewers seems to be: Don't interview until you are well prepared and can evaluate the narrator's comments, and can ask probing questions that elicit further insights and interpretation. Finally, don't use quotes to cover for the lack of explanatory writing the reporter should do.

Welles observed that the failure of the press to scrutinize Reaganomics indicated the "woefully anemic state of such economics reporting in this country." He added,

The economy has become so complex that nearly all economics reporters depend almost exclusively on professional data gatherers and trend forecasters. *Economics reporting has become mainly a process of soliciting opinions from economists*—"'he said, she said' journalism," as *New York Times* columnist Leonard Silk, puts it.[22] [emphasis added]

He further chastized the press for covering supply-side economics "largely by playing quotes and assertions from prominent supply-siders against quotes and assertions from conventional Keynesian economists, and then putting a superficial analytical top-spin on the disparities."[23] He urged more economics writers to "take a long, hard look at the evidence on which those opinions are based." Lamenting the lack of in-depth treatment, he noted that "no reporter to my knowledge has conducted a broad, rigorous investigation and evaluation of the statistical case for supply-side effects."[24]

In exemplary fashion Welles identified significant misuses of the journalistic interview, and referred to using interviews unaided by the support of individual research and evidence gathered by the reporter. He criticized use of the interview not merely as a supplement or complement, but as an alternative to the interviewer's own informed analysis.

Journalists agree on the need for expertise. Helping to evaluate new applicants for Harvard's Nieman Fellowship recently, Mary Ellen Leary commented

[I]t struck me . . . that almost every reporter seeking a year to study at Harvard wanted a background in economics, and expressed . . . great need for it.[25]

Leary, one of the first women named to a Nieman Fellowship, reminisced about her own earlier coverage of the California Legislature. She added that maybe she was "wishing I'd had more economics background" when dealing with legislation on the state's economic issues.

Leary, Welles, and the would-be Nieman Fellows thus joined other journalists and critics who see the need for interviewers to develop substantive knowledge. The interviewer needs the skill to analyze as well as report, and to evoke answers that shed light on significant issues.

The same principle applies to interviewers in all categories: material obtained by interview will be no better than the preparation, training, knowledge, and skill the interviewer brings to bear.

Researchers puzzle about the appropriate circumstances for using interviews as information sources, with all the implied choices and caveats involved. When interviews are the right choice, the next question is how best to cultivate their strengths as research sources, and how to minimize limitations. One promising answer lies in combining interviews with other sources of information, as the following discussion suggests.

COMBINING SOURCES, OR WHAT ELSE IS THERE?

Focus on Examples

Researchers can feel most confident in interviews that provide one method among others, one source among many. The following examples call attention to possible combinations of interviews (and reinterviews) with questionnaires and observation. Other combinations offer simultaneous conduct of interviews and questionnaires with two groups, as well as interviews joined with archives searches and literature surveys. Finally, one person's interviews can be combined with those of others.

Interview, Reinterview, Questionnaire, and Observation

The Teaching Innovation and Evaluation Service (TIES)[26] at the University of California, Berkeley, used a combination of resources to help faculty members who want to improve their teaching. TIES used interviews and reinterviews with teachers and students, along with student questionnaires and classroom observation. Major information sources included staff interviews with teachers designated as "excellent," i.e., who had received Distinguished Teacher Awards and high rankings by their own students who answered evaluative questionnaires.

Lynn Wood, TIES assistant director, explained that interviewers asked the good teachers, "What do you think you do?" The interviews provided ideas, interpretations, and data for the "improving" teachers, whose own students were also asked to answer evaluative questionnaires—after grades had been turned in.

The TIES staff observed classes, developed and interpreted questionnaires from students, and interviewed students, expert teachers, and those working to improve performance. Wood noted changes in the character of the interviews over time. She said the interviewers have become "more directive, more probing, and somewhat 'tougher,'" although respect, confidentiality, and objectivity continued to be strictly observed. Instead of offering standard formats and procedures, the interviewers discussed interpretations and options with teachers seeking to improve. The main objective was to stimulate the teachers' own thinking, and help them find their own way in the rich store of information that the observation, interviews, and questionnaires provide.[27]

Interviews and Questionnaires

One fine-tuned research design specified home interviews conducted with children while their parents simultaneously filled out questionnaires in another room nearby. Writing up the results, Victor Rubin and Elliott A. Medrich reported a completion rate of 87.2 percent, far above that normally expected if questionnaires are delivered and returned by mail.[28] The combined techniques enabled the researchers to increase the informational return from a given expenditure of effort.

The children, for example, were asked about chores, TV-viewing, and out-of-school activities with family members and others. Parents' written questionnaires concerned family demography, socialization, and child-rearing practices. The interviewers were thus free to concentrate on their young narrators, allowing the parents to deal undisturbed with their questionnaires. Further, the two sets of questions broadened the scope of information, obtaining both the child's-eye view and that of the parent.

Interview, Reinterview, and Observation

Mary Ellen Leary used a cluster of techniques to gather data on candidate-media interaction for the book *Phantom Politics,* concerning California's 1974 gubernatorial campaign.[29] In addition to interviews and reinterviews with participants and observers, the project monitored broadcasts and employed "direct participatory observation" in newspaper city rooms and on the campaign trail, where research staff members traveled with candidates and reporters. She also used systematic questionnaires and codified media reports for computer analysis.

One major research technique was "intensive interviewing both with media and . . . candidates, including reinterviewing of the same people at different periods," a procedure that she said proved helpful. This setting allowed participants to respond to specific questions and express their own perceptions. Reinterviews recorded changes in opinions and reactions to new developments as the campaigns progressed. Such perceptions supplemented other material, permitting comparison with the evidence project staff members found through experiences and through questionnaires. Finally, the data could be compared with other information, e.g., the computer analyses of the verbal content of media reports on the campaign.[30]

Interviews, Archive Search, Literature Survey, and Interviews by Others

Interviews can also supplement archival sources and literature review. A current example appears in the book *Across the Border: Rural Development in Mexico and Recent Migration to the United States,* whose authors used both published and unpublished sources in English and Spanish. The latter materials included items from five private archives in Mexico: in San Luis Potosí, and Guadalupe, Trancoso, and Zacatecas.

Interview material came from such sources as:

- "Operation Cooperation," San Diego County, November 1975 to

April 1976, when "special investigators interviewed more than 7,000 employees at several businesses. . . . " The authors noted that "to ensure employer cooperation, confidentiality had to be respected." (p. 93) (Employer preference for undocumented workers.)

• Current Population Survey of 47,000 households that "asks its respondents to indicate their ethnic identity." (p. 153) (Deals with estimates of the illegal population in the US, circa 1975.)

• Oral history interviews in the Bancroft Library, conducted by James W. Wilkie and Edna Monzón de Wilkie. (p. 198), and

• Author-conducted interviews including those with Border Patrol agents; personnel of the Immigration and Naturalization Service (INS); a researcher at the Department of Agricultural Economics, University of California, Berkeley; a member of the Coastal Growers Association; and the Director of PROFAM (p. 198).[31]

Both archival and interview materials were essential in the authors' search for reasons why Mexican migration to the United States has originated principally in one region.

Another example involved interviews that author David Halberstam conducted for his book *The Best and the Brightest* and those conducted by others. Among the sources he considered "unusually valuable" were interviews that Robert Lovett, Henry Luce, Joe Rauh, Dean Acheson, George Kennan, and John Siegenthaler gave for the Kennedy Library.[32] Still another author, Seymour M. Hersh, combined more than a dozen other categories of sources with interviews and reinterviews for his book, *The Price of Power*. The sources included books, newspapers, journals, transcripts of public TV interviews, letters, unpublished manuscripts of other authors, colloquium papers, press statements, sworn statements, court documents, institute proceedings, and congressional and other governmental documents.[33] This scholarly listing emphasized the great value of interviewing, which Hersh found necessary in addition to his access to massive documentation.

CONCLUSION

In deciding when to conduct and/or use interviews, and under what circumstances, again we see the need for critical choices in every decision on their use. If the cost-effectiveness balance is favorable, the timing is appropriate, the interviewer alert and well prepared, and the interview can elicit information not readily available otherwise, then the signal is to go ahead. One can expect effectiveness in obtaining information and have confidence in the material. On the other hand, interviews should be resisted if non-interview sources are likely to be more effective and efficient, timing is dubious, or the interviewer not well prepared.

Finally, when the interview method is seen as the rational and proper choice, seasoned researchers recognize interviews as only one significant element in a cornucopia of research tools. While interviews are occasionally the only method of capturing certain information, even then they are most effective in combination with observation, literature searches, verification, and often the interviews of others.

To say "yes" to the conduct and use of interviews is not always wise. Sometimes, however regretfully, it is better to say "no."

VII

Conclusion

Interviews exert a fascination for researchers, who seek the information, interpretation, opinions, ideas, and clues that skillful interviewers can elicit. Further, researchers find interviews accessible and relatively easy to use. The many virtues of interviews and their vast supply nevertheless signal the need for critical choices and for broadened understanding. To use or quote interview materials naively is to enter a danger zone. The warning signs include failure to consider the ground rules and agreements, the interview setting, the context of the sessions, the participants' agendas, the interviewer's preparation, the narrator's intent, or the role of the editor. While informed performance and use can reward and satisfy all participants, thoughtless or improper use of interviews can at best lower the quality of the outcome, and at worst mean trouble for unwary interviewers, narrators, and users. Choice is the key; to be "well-chosen" is the hallmark of interviews conducted and used appropriately.

To make critical choices wisely, we must avoid blinders that restrict our knowledge to a single slice of the spectrum of interviews. Otherwise we behave like the blind men of the fable, who tested the elephant with their fingertips, and reported on what they experienced: the tail, the ear, the trunk. They "saw" the elephant as a rope, a fan, a snake. Only if a sighted person described the way these elements worked as part of the whole animal could they understand that such a large, intelligent creature existed in its true form and appreciate what it could and could not do.

If all the components of all interviews made up a single creature it would indeed be elephantine, but we as participants and users are not blind;

118

at times we only act that way. We each focus on familiar aspects, and may misinterpret what we experience because we are unaware of all the rest that makes a coherent whole. Each interview is a separate event in a particular style but it can be understood as part of a whole panorama of interview styles and choices that makes as much sense as an elephant does. Understanding both the individual aspects of interviews and their wide range opens the door to discriminating choices.

The researcher's point of view helps to make this clear. Researchers understand the need to evaluate and verify evidence; such tasks are virtually impossible in the vagueness of the term "interview." Consequently, it is a major premise of this analysis that despite some important threads of similarity, all interview styles are not the same. To understand their differences is a first step in making informed choices about both conduct and use.

To make informed choices requires wisdom in this field, and we are indebted to Harlan Cleveland for his concept of the sequence of data that lead to information, knowledge plus theory, and finally, wisdom. The elements of our selected interview types can be recognized as data that are organized to produce information—a semi-finished product. The next step is to put the information to work in the mind where it becomes knowledge, and then integrate it with proposed theories. The result is wisdom or the knowledge to do something, i.e., make critical choices about the conduct and use of interviews.

This search for wisdom leads to high ground so that we can see across several fields of expertise and break out of the compartments of the one or two fields we each know. Professional practitioners well understand the types of interviews they use. It is less clear, however, how well the interviewer or participant who knows one type of interview understands and appreciates the other types, or how to choose among them. Further, those with interests less focused—researchers, writers, readers, and narrators—may give little or no thought to how vague the unmodified term "interview" really is, and how little information that familiar term conveys.

While some researchers and writers distinguish among types of interviews, others seem unclear about a variety of ground rules and principles, perhaps criticizing or disdaining one type for not being something different. Some historians accept written memoirs, but question the value of oral history interviews, presumably because they are based on individuals' words that are originally spoken rather than committed to paper. Further, some scholars studying current issues hesitate to use journalistic interviews as research sources, despite the abundance of suggestions they can provide. The result is muddle.

On the other hand, the writer has seen a variety of research proposals that include "interviews," but lack rationales, justification, or clear understanding of the choices presented in the panorama of interview options. Perhaps interviews are becoming both dubious sources and "automatic" resources, catch-alls, unacceptable to some as forms of research, while embraced uncritically by others. Only a vague, ambiguous, and undifferentiated concept could be at the same time so popular and so suspect.

The difference between using and misusing interview types lies in knowing what each is, evaluating it, and deciding how best to use it. The scholar could use the journalistic interview as a source of clues, an alerting device to stimulate further research. The historian could (and does) use the oral history interview as an individual's personal statement to be verified by other evidence. The researcher could profit by weighing the trade-offs between a survey of hundreds of local government officials, and a few extended scholarly interviews with selected narrators.

This discussion approached the study of interviews in three major steps. First, to test the assumption that all interviews are not the same, four interview types were identified and their intrinsic differences and similarities examined. Next, because interviews are events before they become documents or data, three major principles involved in the conduct and use of all interview types were formulated, and their application and the consequences of their use examined. Finally, the roles and responsibilities of participants and users of different types of interviews were investigated. The analysis also considered whether and when to interview, and presented examples to illuminate the interview experience.

Major interview types were designated as (1) survey research and polling, (2) journalistic, (3) scholarly research, and (4) oral history. Principles were identified as control and flexibility, ethics, and techniques, and were observed as they formed and applied to each interview type. Participants who bring interviews to life were identified as the interviewer, narrator, the researcher, the editor and publisher, and the ultimate reader or user. These categories were formulated by the writer. While some appear self-evident, others may seem arbitrary, and readers are invited to challenge or improve on any or all of them.

To keep the discussion linked to the world of experience, examples illustrated typical or unique circumstances as well as specific problems. Those examples of activities analogous to interviews—e.g., byline articles and other published writings that bear an individual's name—were included to demonstrate how conclusions with respect to interviews may also apply in other related fields.

The matrix consisting of four interview types, five participants, and three principles was designed to help identify the opportunities, responsibilities, and options characteristic of each type of interview. While the matrix introduces important elements, they stay in place only briefly. When the matrix is established and each slot filled, the players may begin to move about. One person may adopt new roles; an interviewer trained for one role may change hats and conduct several types of interviews. If the conclusions and principles are valid, however, an actor can step into each new setting, review the stage directions, and function effectively in the new role. Moreover, the researcher and final user can identify the scene, the setting, and rules for each interview type, regardless of who fills the role, and can evaluate the outcome before making a choice.

Cutting across the categories and types of interviews, principles, and roles of participants is the ever-present politics of the interview—the interplay of interests that must be served. The interviewer may want to discover as much of the story as possible; the narrator may have a point to make or details to conceal; and the researcher may be searching for data to analyze and verify for evidence to support an argument. The user may see the results raw, or as transmuted by the researcher, and may read for information, fun, profit, or simply to satisfy curiosity. Finally, the editor and/or publisher, who assigns and will dispose of the interview, may be guided by the need to publish the most, first.

The interviewer shows how interests are expressed through techniques. In survey research or polling, the interviewer has no need or chance to push for unique material or information beyond the interview schedule. On the other hand, a journalistic interviewer may hope to "pick the lock," and may be looking particularly for the unrevealed, unusual, idiosyncratic, or startling. In the scholarly research interview, the driving interest is to find useful material relating to the research topic. Unrelated details would usually be edited out or left unused. Finally, the interest of the oral history interviewer is that of a facilitator, who encourages the narrator in what he or she wants to say, limited only by the focus of the topic series involved. In sum, all interests are served by the interviewer's good preparation, effective rapport with the narrator, and attentive listening.

The principle of control demonstrates how interests can clash or coincide, and evokes the significance of ethics and techniques. With respect to ethical standards, we have observed how easy it is to find agreement on overall desirability, and how hard to agree on specifics. Implementing ethical standards and applying sanctions is hardest of all. In general, ethical codes seemed to avoid the notion of punishing infractions.

While interviewers can refer to their own codes of ethics, narrators and respondents have virtually no external guidance. Even when codes are available, personal awareness and judgment remain the last resort in the sensitive area of ethical issues. Thus the researcher evaluating an interview must search for clues on ethical behavior and remain alert to what can happen when ethics go awry.

Editors, publishers, and researchers are sometimes slighted in analyses of interviews. These roles, nevertheless, are powerful, and the discussion has sought to focus attention on the actors. Currently, editors are occasionally accused of taking too little responsibility, e.g., failing to require verification of an interview's accuracy, or to ascertain the name of an interviewer's otherwise anonymous source. In such cases, editors are seen as failing in leadership, if they do not hold interviewers and columnists to standards of accuracy, or if they neglect significant questions that could reveal carelessness or fraud. Editors are also sometimes blamed for exerting undue pressure on interviewers to get a story ahead of the competition, and to make it dramatic and entertaining. The shadow of a double standard for the editor and for the interviewer is in part lifted when the interests of the researcher and the reader are protected through publication of appropriate corrections where necessary.

Everyone—including the narrator and final user—gains from a clear understanding of interview styles and options. Perhaps the researcher stands to gain most by making critical choices wisely. To determine the most appropriate interview type, the researcher may weigh options, e.g., the ability to elicit trends and assemble numerical data in survey research, as compared with seeking through scholarly research interviews the individual perceptions of persons on the cutting edge of knowledge. Will more telling information emerge from the challenge of the journalistic interview, or from the more gently evoked associations and perceptions of oral history? Since specialized training is usually needed for these kinds of interviews, the researcher may need to hire a practitioner as interviewer, or at least obtain reliable advice and instruction before trying to step into the role.

The considerations and choices noted here suggest ways to avoid costly and time-consuming efforts that lead to frustration and waste. To see interviews as clusters of choices should help researchers and other participants identify the possibilities and options open to them. To choose well among alternatives is as important as implementing that choice effectively.

Thus choice is the fulcrum for exercising the powers of interviews, and choices abound. One can choose whether or how to conduct or use interviews; choose the type and evaluate its integrity by the ways control, ethics, and techniques are applied; and choose whether to accept or reject the performance of interviewer, narrator, researcher, or editor. Wise choices can and should be made—that is the goal of this study, which is strongly spurred by advocacy.

Interviews are a virtually inexhaustible source of human understanding: facts, interpretations, viewpoints, perceptions, and memories. Much of what we know we learn from each other through question and answer. Interviews—what others can tell us—are precious, renewable human resources that will repay all the wit and wisdom we can muster to cultivate them and protect them from misuse, and harvest their never-ending abundance.

Notes

Chapter I

1. For a fine capsule history of the interview and a satisfying guide to journalistic interviewing, see John Brady, *The Craft of Interviewing* (New York, N.Y.: Vintage Books, 1977). The history is the Appendix, pp. 220-232. See especially p. 220. Hereafter, *The Craft of Interviewing*.

2. Mary Ellen Leary, letter to the writer, September 20, 1984. As a member of the reading committee who commented on and evaluated an earlier draft of this paper, she provided thoughtful comments and ideas as well as suggestions for fresh material. The writer gratefully acknowledges these valuable contributions and has used many of them. Hereafter, these quotes and items will be identified as "Leary, 1984."

3. In this connection, Robin W. Winks, ed., has prepared *The Historian as Detective: Essays on Evidence* (New York, N.Y.: Harper Colophon Books, 1968), a witty guide to verification. It is recommended not only for historians alone, but for the whole community of researchers.

4. The eventual consumer may enter the interview chain at several points, before the researcher begins to work on the material or after the researcher's work is completed; before the editor has reworked or rearranged the interview, or after editing, cutting or interpretations are in place.

The oral history interview provides an example. After the oral history interview has been transcribed, as at The Bancroft Library, it is lightly edited by the interviewer, reviewed and approved by the narrator, final-typed, bound and deposited in a research library. Anyone with a legitimate interest in the interview may read it, under the conditions established by the narrator and the Library.

Such a reader has a virtually pristine report, as spoken by the narrator. In turn, the reader may search for background only, or read from general interest and write nothing based on the interview, thus leaving no imprint on the material, taking the place at the end of the interview line.

Another researcher may gain access for research purposes and use the interview and the quotations it provides for articles, books, or other documents, as long as the narrator's conditions are met (e.g., the material is not sealed, permission for extensive quotes is obtained). Before this researcher's material is published and it reaches the ultimate reader, a process of selection and editing may change both the quantity and quality of the presentation. Further, certain elements may be lost, such as explanations of guidelines and style that are essential to a full understanding of the interview methodology and its significance. The danger is that the ultimate reader may unknowingly experience loss of content and interpretation so that the integrity of the interview is altered or weakened.

5. Re: substantiation, Ben H. Bagdikian, presently Dean of the Graduate School of Journalism, UCB, journalist and author, in letter to the writer, August 15, 1984. Bagdikian, as a member of the reading committee, commented on an earlier draft of this study, and generously offered additional material from his own experience. The writer gratefully acknowledges this help. Hereafter citations are identified as "Bagdikian, 1984."

6. Jack Leister, Head Librarian, Institute of Governmental Studies, conversation with the writer, January 2, 1985.

7. "Libel Suits Show News Approaches of Papers, TV and Magazines Differ," *New York Times,* January 31, 1985, p. 13, quoting Everette E. Dennis, executive director, Gannett Center for Media Studies, Columbia University.

8. "Forum: Can the Press Tell the Truth?" *Harper's Magazine* 270(1616): 37-51 (January 1985), p. 48.

9. Harlan Cleveland, *The Knowledge Executive: Leadership in an Information Society* (New York, N.Y.: E. P. Dutton, 1985). See the excerpt, "Information as a Resource," *The Saybrook Perspective* (Fall 1985), pp. 2-6, especially p. 3.

10. See Webster's *New World Dictionary of the American Language,* 2nd College ed., David B. Guralnik, ed.-in-chief (Cleveland, Oh.: William Collins Publishing, Inc., 1980), p. 1130.

Chapter II

1. Robert L. Kahn and Charles F. Cannell, *The Dynamics of Interviewing: Theory, Technique and Cases* (New York, N.Y.: John Wiley & Sons, Inc., 1957), p. vi.

2. See *The Craft of Interviewing;* see especially chapters 4 and 5.

3. Leary, 1984.

4. See, for example, *Interviewer's Manual,* rev. ed. (Ann Arbor, Mich.: Survey Research Center, Institute for Social Research, The University of Michigan, 1976), p. 1.

5. Ibid., p. 2.

6. See, e.g., *The American Heritage Dictionary of the English Language,* William Morris, ed. (Boston, Mass.: Houghton Mifflin Co., 1969), p. 1015.

7. In a two-pronged approach, the federal census seeks to achieve both a 100 percent count of the population (short form) and a 20 percent sample (long form). Those included in the sample receive a long form that also includes the short form questions.

Ilona Einowski, Data Archivist, State Data Program, Survey Research Center, UCB, provided the explanation (February 1982).

8. Jean Atkinson, *Handbook for Interviewers,* Office of Population Censuses and Surveys, Social Survey Division (London, England: Her Majesty's Stationery Office, 1971), p. 3.

9. Ibid., p. 50.

10. Leary, 1984. "Not all journalistic interviews are confrontational. Sometimes (if trying to illustrate to readers what an ass somebody is) you make an effort to quote him exactly. With tapes, this is easier. It can be quite revealing to carry precise language . . . not tone it down or dress it up. It's a recognized journalistic technique."

11. Promotional mailing from *The Washington Monthly*, received in Berkeley, January 1982.

12. Story, "New Limits . . . " datelined Washington, was a *Los Angeles Times* article appearing in the *San Francisco Chronicle*, January 16, 1982, p. 10.

The *Chronicle* also carried a *New York Times* article with a Washington dateline March 1, 1985, p. 17: "State Dept. 'Punishes' N.Y. Reporter for Story." It began:

The director of the State Department's Bureau of Politico-Military Affairs has ordered his staff not to talk to a *New York Times* correspondent Leslie H. Gelb, who wrote that the United States had contingency plans for placing nuclear weapons in Canada, Iceland, Bermuda and Puerto Rico.

The article said that earlier Secretary of State George Schultz had asked the *Times* not to publish it. "The *Times* told Schultz then that security was not at issue because the information had already been printed in foreign countries."

13. "Critical Health Official Transferred," *San Francisco Chronicle*, March 3, 1984, p. 6.

14. Lacey Fosburgh, Assistant Professor, Graduate School of Journalism, UCB, unpublished memo shown to the writer, February 19, 1981. Quotes from this Fosburgh interview hereafter are cited as Fosburgh, 1981.

15. See Edwin R. Bayley, *Joe McCarthy and the Press* (Madison, Wis.: The University of Wisconsin Press, 1981), p. 68.

16. Ibid., p. 70.

17. Ibid., p. 218.

18. Anna Starcke, *Survival: Taped interviews with South Africa's power élite* (Capetown, South Africa: Tafelberg Publishers, Ltd., 1978), p. 62. Hereafter, Starcke, *Survival*.

19. Stanley Scott, *Governing California's Coast* (Berkeley, Calif.: Institute of Governmental Studies, University of California, 1975). Hereafter, *Governing California's Coast*.

20. Based on discussions with Stanley Scott, assistant director, Institute of Governmental Studies, University of California, Berkeley, 1981.

21. Robert N. Bellah, Richard Madsen, William M. Sullivan, Ann Swidler, and Steven M. Tipton, *Habits of the Heart: Individualism and Commitment in American Life* (Berkeley, Calif.: University of California Press, 1985). See Appendix, "Social Science as Public Philosophy," esp. pp. 303-305. Also see Preface note 2, p. 309, for descriptions of interview technique.

22. Willa K. Baum, *Oral History for the Local Historical Society*, 2nd ed. rev. (Nashville, Tenn.: American Association for State and Local History, 1971), p. 7.

23. Loc. cit.

24. See brochure, *Oral History at The Bancroft Library* (Berkeley, Calif.: Regional Oral History Office, The Bancroft Library, University of California, n.d.). Hereafter, *Oral History at The Bancroft Library*.

25. See James W. Wilkie and Edna Monzón de Wilkie, eds., *Elitelore as a New Field of Inquiry: Influences of the Novel, Film and Oral History on National Policy Decisions in Latin America*. Reprint Series (U.C.), Pacific Basin Economic Study Center, 1979.

The Wilkies give their assessment of elitelore: "Memoirs of leaders reveal how they have selected information for themselves and for public consumption to protect their egos and to develop a myth about themselves, myth calculated to give everlasting life to their ideas." p. vi.

Seeking to differentiate aspects of nonelitelore, they coin the mouth-filling "popularlore," as follows: " . . . popularlore is the unique biographical aspect of the lore of the common man as it has been tape recorded by a few scholars such as Oscar Lewis; folklore is seen as the generalized or typological analysis that emerges from the synthesizing of individual cases." p. 80.

26. See interviews reported in John Langston Gwaltney, *Drylongso: A Self-Portrait of Black America* (New York, N.Y.: Random House, 1980).

27. Him Mark Lai, Genny Lim, and Judy Yung, *Island: Poetry and History of Chinese Immigrants on Angel Island, 1910-1940* [San Francisco, Calif.: HOC DOI (History of Chinese Detained on Island) a project of the Chinese Culture Foundation of San Francisco, 1980]. Hereafter, *Island.*

28. Ronald Blythe, *The View in Winter: Reflections on Old Age* (New York: Harcourt Brace Jovanovich, 1979).

29. Ronald J. Grele, ed., *Envelopes of Sound: Six Practitioners Discuss the Method, Theory and Practice of Oral History and Oral Testimony* (Chicago, Ill.: Precedent Publishing, Inc., 1975), p. 135. Hereafter, *Envelopes of Sound.*

30. Studs Terkel, *Hard Times: An Oral History of the Great Depression* (New York, N.Y.: Pocket Books, 1970).

31. Irving Louis Horowitz, ed., *Constructing Policy: Dialogues with Social Scientists in the National Political Arena* (New York, N.Y.: Praeger Publishers, 1979), p. v.

32. Ibid., p. 13.

33. Ibid., p. 14.

34. Wilfrid Sheed, "The Interview as Art," in *The Good Word and Other Words* (New York, N.Y.: E. P. Dutton, 1978) (hereafter "Interview as Art"), discusses *The Paris Review Interviews,* Vol. IV. See p. 210.

35. Ibid., p. 211.

36. Loc. cit.

Chapter III

1. Sissela Bok, *Lying: Moral Choice in Public and Private Life* (New York, N.Y.: Vintage Books, 1979), p. 260. Hereafter, *Lying.* The writer is indebted to Ben H. Bagdikian for recommending this book.

2. Definition of "plagiarize," *The American Heritage Dictionary of the English Language* (New York, N.Y.: American Heritage Publishing Co., 1969), p. 1001.

3. Leary, 1984.

4. *Governing California's Coast,* p. xviii.

5. Ibid., p. xix.

6. Rufus P. Browning, Dale Rogers Marshall, David H. Tabb, *Protest is Not Enough: The Struggle of Blacks and Hispanics for Equality in Urban Politics* (Berkeley, Calif.: University of California Press, 1984), "Acknowledgments" p. xv. See also Appendix B, "Data," pp. 268-271 and Appendix C, "Indices and Measures," pp. 272-287.

7. *Oral History at The Bancroft Library.*

8. Observation by the writer during oral history interviews with Katherine A. Towle, 1969.

9. Observation by the writer during oral history interviews with Ewald T. Grether, 1975-86.

10. Observation by the writer during oral history interviews with Mary Ellen Leary, 1980. Also Leary, 1984.

11. "Walter Gordon, Athlete, Officer in Law Enforcement and Administration, Governor of the Virgin Islands," vol. 1, oral history interviews conducted 1976, 1977, 1978, 1979 by Anne H. Brower, Edward Farris, Amelia Fry, Rosemary Levenson, and Caryn Price, Regional Oral History Office, The Bancroft Library, 1980. Preface, Anne H. Brower, p. ii.

12. Hugh Trevor-Roper, *Hermit of Peking: The Hidden Life of Sir Edmund Backhouse* (New York, N.Y.: Alfred A. Knopf, 1977), p. 234. It is sobering to note that even as good a sleuth as Hugh Trevor-Roper later had trouble with questions of authenticity. He was quoted as saying at first that the so-called "Hitler Diary," "found" in 1983 seemed to be the real thing, an opinion he later reversed.

13. Ibid., p. 245. For a discussion of institutional lying, see Anthony Marro, "When the Government Tells Lies," *Columbia Journalism Review* 29-41 (March-April 1985).

14. Laura Longley Babb, ed. *Of the press, by the press (And others, too)* (Washington Post Writers Group, 1974). Hereafter, *Of the press.*

Misquotes, among other problems of journalistic interviews, are widely deplored both by readers and news professionals. Journalistic self-examination appears in *Of the press.* It is a critical study of the inside workings of the news business and is based on the "news pages, editorials, columns and internal staff memos of *The Washington Post.*" (title page)

Candid and valuable, the book treats problems of misquotes, leaks, anonymous sources, pre-trial publicity, advocacy, and conflicts of interest. Babb's presentation and examples form the basis for much of the interpretation and characterization discussed below.

15. Ibid., p. 132.

16. Ibid., pp. 109-110.

17. See Betty Medsger, "Trial by Newspaper," *New West* (renamed *California Monthly*) 126, 127, 130-132 (November 19, 1979), hereafter, "Trial by Newspaper"; Preble Stolz, *Judging Judges: The Investigation of Rose Bird and the California Supreme Court* (New York, N.Y.: Free Press, 1981), especially the Appendix Chronology, pp. 429-436; Betty Medsger, *Framed: The New Right Attack on Chief Justice Rose Bird and the Courts* (Long Island City, N.Y.: Pilgrim Press, 1983), hereafter, *Framed: The New Right Attack;* Betty Medsger, "Framed," *feed/back* 26-33, 46-47 (Fall 1983), subhead: "An Excerpt from a New Book Sheds Light on the Los Angeles Times' Role in the Confirmation of State Supreme Court Justice Rose Bird"; and Richard Thomson, "Bird vs. Clark, Revisited: Two books, two views of the high-court political battle," *California Journal* 421-424, 434 (November 1983).

18. Medsger, "Trial by Newspaper."

19. Ibid.

20. Some credence is given to these queries by the 1985 campaign to unseat Chief Justice Bird and Justices Cruz Reynoso, Joseph Grodin, and Stanley Mosk, whose terms are also up for renewal. The campaign gained impetus when Governor George Deukmejian charged that the court was anti-business, and encouraged voters to act accordingly. See the *San Francisco Chronicle,* "Court Decisions: Governor Tells Why Bird Is Bad For Business," Steve Wiegand, February 14, 1985, p. 1.

21. Fosburgh, interview, May 11, 1982.

22. Interview with Edwin R. Bayley, Dean of the Graduate School of Journalism, UCB, January 22, 1981. Hereafter, Bayley, 1981.

23. Bagdikian, 1984.

128

24. Bayley, 1981.

25. Ed Salzman, Capitol Bureau Chief, *Sacramento Bee,* conversation with the writer, January 27, 1984. Salzman, former editor of the *California Journal,* in 1985 became editor and publisher of *Golden State Report: The magazine of politics and public policy in California.*

26. Thomson, "Journalistic Ethics: Some Probings by a Media Keeper," *Nieman Reports* 7-14 (Winter-Spring 1978), see p. 11. The writer is indebted to William B. Arthur, executive director of the National News Council, for providing the Thomson article.

27. Leary, 1984.

28. Mervin D. Field, telephone interviews with the writer, October 16 and 22, 1981. Hereafter, Field interview(s).

29. Theodora Kroeber, *Ishi in Two Worlds: A Biography of the Last Wild Indian in North America* (Berkeley, Calif.: University of California Press, 1967), pp. 127-128, 135. Hereafter *Ishi.*

30. *Ishi,* pp. 127-129.

31. Ibid., p. 135.

32. Norman Cousins, "Press Sometimes Abuses Its Power," *The Masthead,* 29(4): 3-5 (Winter 1977), see p. 5.

33. Dean Acheson, *Present at the Creation: My Years in the State Department* (New York, N.Y.: W. W. Norton & Company, Inc., 1969), p. 764.

34. Loc. cit.

35. *Of the press,* pp. 18-19.

36. Patricia Lynch, "Is Lyndon LaRouche using *your* name? How the LaRouchians masquerade as journalists to gain information," *Columbia Journalism Review* 42-46 (March-April 1985), see p. 42.

37. Ibid., p. 43.

38. Wallace J. S. Johnson, "Berkeley: Twelve Years as the Nation in Microcosm, 1962-1974," Harriet Nathan and Stanley Scott, eds., *Experiment and Change in Berkeley: Essays on City Politics 1950-1975* (Berkeley, Calif.: Institute of Governmental Studies, University of California, 1978), pp. 179-230. See especially pp. 195-196.

39. Ibid., p. 196.

40. Leary, 1984.

41. See Theodore M. Becker and Peter R. Meyers, "Empathy and Bravado: Interviewing Reluctant Bureaucrats," *The Public Opinion Quarterly* 38(4): 605-613 (Winter 1974-75), p. 611.

42. Ibid., p. 605.

43. Ibid., p. 608.

44. Ibid., p. 613, note 20.

45. Leary, 1984.

46. Fosburgh, 1981.

47. See "Oral History Association approves adoption of Wingspread Guidelines," *The Recorder,* March 1980, pp. 3-4.

48. Karen J. Winkler, "Oral History: Coming of Age in the 1980's," *The Chronicle of Higher Education,* October 14, 1980, p. 3.

49. Loc. cit.

50. From *Freedom Accuracy Fairness: The National News Council,* brochure courtesy of William B. Arthur. Hereafter, *Freedom Accuracy Fairness.* See also Patrick Brogan, *Spiked: The Short Life and Death of the National News Council,* A Twentieth Century Fund Paper (New York, N.Y.: Priority Press Publications, 1985), p. v, Foreword by M. J. Rossant, Director.

51. *Freedom Accuracy Fairness.*

52. Letter from William B. Arthur, to the writer, October 9, 1980.

53. Ibid.

54. Ibid.

55. Bruce M. Swain, *Reporters' Ethics* (Ames, Ohio: The Ohio State University Press, 1978), pp. 92 and 93. Hereafter, *Reporters' Ethics.*

56. Ibid.

57. See Bernard Rubin, ed., *Questioning Media Ethics* (New York, N.Y.: Praeger Publishers, Praeger Special Studies, 1978), note, p. 13. The citation on the reversal is to *The Capital Times Company,* 223 NLRB, no. 87, 1976.

58. *Reporters' Ethics,* Appendices, pp. 111-134.

As originally stated or amended, the codes include the American Society of Newspaper Editors Statement of Principles (October 23, 1975); Associated Press Managing Editors Association Code of Ethics (April 15, 1975); Society of Professional Journalists, Sigma Delta Chi, Code of Ethics (1973); *Chicago Sun-Times* and *Daily News* Code of Professional Standards (October 1, 1974); *Des Moines Register* and *Tribune* Code of Ethics (June 1975); *Louisville Courier-Journal* and *Times* Policy and Outside Work of News, Editorial, and Photo Department Staff Members (June 27, 1977) *The Louisville Courier-Journal and Times Company*—Conflict of Interest and Management Personnel (January 21, 1975); *Milwaukee Journal* Rules and Guidelines (October 5, 1973); Scripps-Howard Newspapers Principles and Practices for All Personnel (revised September 1976); and *Washington Post* Standards and Ethics (November 1977).

In Swain's ten-code sample, five discussed some abstract concepts and did so both in general and in specific terms. For example the ASNE statement provided that:

> Journalists should respect the rights of people involved in the news, observe the common standards of decency and stand accountable to the public for the fairness and accuracy of their news reports. (Swain, p. 112)

For a recent examination of attitudes toward codes of ethics, see Ed Remitz, "To Code or Not to Code," SPJ/SDX Convention, *feed/back* 37-41, 53 (Fall, 1983). Remitz sums it up: "A survey by *feed/back* finds only a consensus of disagreement among editors and executives at major California newspapers, along with union and academic observers." The points of view are presented clearly, the questions are familiar. "Should there be such codes? If so, what should they stipulate? Should their structures be advisory or enforceable? Should ethical criteria be considered in the pursuit of awards?" (p. 37).

59. The codes spelled out positions concerning acceptance of items of value—freebies—that are offered to reporters. These include meals, travel, tickets to events, gifts, books, records, and club memberships. Other activities that may generate conflict of interest include outside employment and business and civic involvements. The issue focuses on whether the item in question would compromise or influence a reporter's coverage. Abstaining from even the appearance of wrongdoing seems to be the most general recommendation.

60. Bagdikian, 1984.

61. Thelma F. Batten, *Reasoning and Research: A Guide for Social Science Methods* (Boston, Mass.: Little, Brown and Company, 1971). Hereafter, *Reasoning and Research.* See p. 207. The writer is indebted to Beatrice M. Bain for this reference.

62. Robert T. Bower and Priscilla de Gasparis, *Ethics in Social Research: Protecting the Interests of Human Subjects* (New York, N.Y.: Praeger Publisher, 1978), p. 37.

63. Ibid., p. 72.

64. Field interview, October 22, 1981.

65. *A Guide to Professional Ethics in Political Science,* ed. Richard F. Schier

(Washington, D.C.: The American Political Science Association, 1985), p. 8.
    66. *Reasoning and Research,* pp. 209-210.
    67. Bagdikian, 1984.
    68. *Lying,* p. 263.

Chapter IV

    1. Fosburgh, 1981.
    2. See Timothy Crouse, *The Boys on the Bus* (New York, N.Y.: Random House, 1973).
    3. Theodore H. White, *In Search of History: A Personal Adventure* (New York, N.Y.: Warner Books, 1978), p. 196.
    4. See *Media Performance in Political Campaigns* (draft working paper), report of a conference, 1977, sponsored by the Institute of Governmental Studies and the Graduate School of Journalism, University of California, Berkeley; the *California Journal;* and the Department of Communication, Stanford University (Berkeley, Calif.: Institute of Governmental Studies, University of California, 1978). Hereafter, *Media Performance.* See Tillinghast, p. 18.
    5. See David S. Broder, *Changing of the Guard: Power and Leadership in America* (New York, N.Y.: Simon and Schuster, 1980), "Acknowledgments," p. 483. Hereafter, *Changing of the Guard.*
    6. *Changing of the Guard,* p. 466.
    7. Ibid., p. 481.
    8. Bagdikian, 1984. In addition, Mary Ellen Leary warned against placing all the burden for an unproductive interview on the interviewer, since even able and experienced people may be unresponsive as narrators. She said that when the narrator was slow-witted or noncommunicative, her impulse was "to get out fast and wash my hands of the whole thing." Patience, however, may pay off, "because often a narrator needs time to establish confidence, or quicken memory, or re-establish himself back in to the topic at hand, away from his present scene." (Leary, 1984.)
    9. Fosburgh, 1981.
    10. See *Channels,* October/November 1981 issue; p. 3 for the Moyers letter.
    11. Seymour M. Hersh, *The Price of Power: Kissinger in the Nixon White House* (New York, N.Y. Summit Books, 1983), notes to Chapter 18, see p. 652. Hereafter, *The Price of Power.* See also Chapter 2, "The Unnamed Source," in David Shaw, *Press Watch: A Provocative Look at How Newspapers Report the News* (New York, N.Y.: Macmillan Publishing Company, 1984), pp. 52-85. He discussed the way the press and TV media sometimes oppose and sometimes acquiesce in, or even volunteer "background" and "non-attribution" status for information they use. He noted that

> Several years ago, when the American Society of Newspaper Editors polled its members on the problem of stories with unidentified sources, 81 percent said that unnamed sources are less believable than named sources.
> But 28 percent of the editors in the survey requested that they not be quoted by name. (p. 85)

For a revealing discussion of the problem of judging accuracy of quoted statements when both narrators and the concerns of the interviewer are identified, see "Journalism, History and Journalistic History—An Exchange," *New York Times Book Review,* December 16, 1984, pp. 28-29. Discussants included Secretary of Defense Caspar W. Weinberger, Theodore Draper (who reviewed Strobe Talbott's book *Deadly Gambits*), arms negotiator Paul H. Nitze, and Talbott.

The writer is indebted to Dorothy C. Tompkins for this and many other useful clippings and references.

12. Leary, by phone, 1985.

13. Mary Ellen Leary, "A Journalists's Perspective: Government and Politics in California and the Bay Area," an oral history conducted in 1979 by Harriet Nathan, Regional Oral History Office, The Bancroft Library, University of California, Berkeley, 1981, 225p. See p. 61. Hereafter, Leary, oral history.

She later observed that some narrators will say, "Well, let's start out off the record and then agree on what you can quote." She speculated that the ploy might be "a defensive guard put up when the narrator isn't sure how hot the going will get." (Leary, 1984.)

14. Leary, oral history, p. 95.

15. See Katherine A. Towle, "Administration and Leadership," an oral history conducted 1967 by Harriet Nathan, Regional Oral History Office, The Bancroft Library, University of California, Berkeley, 1970, 304p. See p. 219.

16. Loc. cit.

17. David Halberstam, *The Best and the Brightest* (New York, N.Y.: Random House, 1972), pp. 668-669. Hereafter, *The Best and the Brightest*.

18. Loc. cit.

19. Starcke, *Survival*. p. 63.

20. Ibid., p. 126.

21. Oriana Fallaci, *Limelighters* (London, England: Michael Joseph, 1968). Fallaci calls these items "monologues provoked by my questions or opinions." (p. x) See the interviews with Fellini, p. 55; Bergman, 38; Magnani, 197; and Connery, 210. On the interview page that reported the Fellini exchange, Fallaci's questions/comments occupied 26 lines, Fellini's replies, 9 lines. This example is at one extreme: in another interview at the other end of the spectrum, Fallaci's questions occupied 7 lines, while Geraldine Chaplin's answers (p. 178) filled 28 lines. Fallaci appeared to encourage Chaplin.

22. See Wilfrid Sheed in the 1976 essay-review, "Interview as Art," pp. 206-211. He comments on the series, *Writers at Work: The Paris Review Interviews,* Fourth series. See p. 207.

23. See *Writers at Work: The Paris Review Interviews,* Fifth Series, George Plimpton, ed. (New York, N.Y.: The Viking Press, 1981), p. 362.

24. *Writers at Work: The Paris Review Interviews,* Sixth Series, George Plimpton, ed., Introduction by Frank Kermode (New York, N.Y.: The Viking Press, 1984), p. x.

25. See *Conversations with Writers II,* Vol. 3 (A Bruccoli Clark Book) (Detroit, Mich.: Gale Research Company, 1978), p. 49.

26. Irving Louis Horowitz, ed., *Constructing Policy: Dialogues with Social Scientists in the National Political Arena* (New York, N.Y.: Praeger Publishers, 1979), pp. v and vi.

27. Bayley interview, January 22, 1981.

28. William B. Arthur, letter to the writer, October 9, 1980.

29. Ibid.

30. David Halberstam, *The Powers That Be* (New York, N.Y.: Alfred A. Knopf, 1979), p. 740. Hereafter, *The Powers That Be.*

31. John Scott and Eliska Chanlett, *Planning the Research Interview,* Laboratories for Population Statistics, Manual Series No. 4 (Chapel Hill, N.C.: University of North Carolina, 1973), pp. 17-18.

32. Kathleen Gerson, *Hard Choices: How Women Decide about Work, Career,*

and Motherhood (Berkeley, Calif.: University of California Press, 1985), p. 245.

33. See Howard Schuman and Stanley Presser's study *Questions and Answers in Attitude Surveys: Experiments on Question Form, Wording, and Context* (New York, N.Y.: Academic Press, Inc., 1981) discussed in *ISR Newsletter* (Institute for Social Research, University of Michigan, Spring/Summer 1982), "Questions and Answers," see p. 6.

34. Ibid., p. 7.

35. See "HUD's Homeless Study Questioned," Bob English, *UC Clip Sheet,* 60 (4) (August 21, 1984).

36. Bagdikian, *Media Performance,* p. 150.

37. Field interview, October 22, 1981.

38. See William L. Nicholls, II, George A. Lavender, and J. Merrill Shanks *Berkeley SRC CATI: An Overview of Berkeley SRC CATI, Version 1,* Survey Research Center Working Paper 31 (Berkeley, Calif.: University of California, February 1980), pp. 1 and 2.

39. Field interview, October 22, 1981.

40. Jean M. Converse and Howard Schuman, *Conversations at Random: Survey Research as Interviewers See It* (New York, N.Y.: John Wiley & Sons, Inc., 1974), p. 77. Hereafter, *Conversations at Random.*

41. Loc. cit.

42. Seymour Sudman and Norman M. Bradburn, *Response Effects in Surveys: a Review and Synthesis* (Chicago, Ill.: Aldine Publishing Co., 1974) (copyright, National Opinion Research Center), p. 5.

43. Allen D. Grimshaw, "Language as Obstacle and as Data in Sociological Research," *Items* 23 (2): 17-12 (June 1969), Social Science Research Council. See p. 21.

44. *Conversations at Random,* pp. 62-63.

45. With respect to narrators' benefits in a variety of interviews, the writer is indebted to psychologist and educator Verneice Thompson for a useful view by Nevitt Sanford, in "Social Psychology: Its Place in Personology," *American Psychologist* 37 (8): 896-903 (August 1982), p. 897. Sanford's view of benefits included the chance to say things "for which there had not previously been an appropriate audience," and to state ideas and thoughts that had been only vague earlier. "When these are met with attention and interest, self-esteem rises." He also noted the chance for narrators to "reflect on their lives, to take stock, to think out loud about alternatives." He added that through interviews "Professors often gain some self-insight and become more open to the psychological needs of students."

Sanford's comments referred to the role of interviews in psychology, a significant field that this paper does not address, but one that reflects similarity of effects across fields.

46. Field interview, October 22, 1981.

47. Cover letter included in mailing from *Public Opinion,* published by the American Enterprise Institute for Public Policy Research, Washington, DC (received November 1981).

48. Ibid., enclosed brochure, *There's Not Another Magazine Like It In the World.*

49. Mary Ellen Leary, *Phantom Politics: Campaigning in California* (Washington, DC: Public Affairs Press, 1977), p. 124. Hereafter, *Phantom Politics.*

50. Ibid., p. 123.

51. Ibid., p. 124.

52. Field, *Media Performance,* p. 41.

53. Post, *Media Performance,* pp. 117, 118. At the time of his discussion, Rollin Post was the editor of "Newsroom," on Channel 9, KQED, San Francisco. He was the

only exclusively political reporter in California television.

54. *Phantom Politics,* p. 172.

55. Miller, *Media Performance,* p. 44.

56. See E. J. Dionne, Jr., "Polling: A Growth Industry With Problems," in "Viewpoint," *San Francisco Examiner and Chronicle,* March 2, 1980, magazine p. 24, article reprinted from the *New York Times.*

57. Ibid.

58. Reeves, *Media Performance,* p. 84.

59. Miller, *Media Performance,* pp. 47 and 48.

60. Beatrice M. Bain, letter to the writer, 1984.

61. Interview with Stanley Scott, Institute of Governmental Studies, May 21, 1981 and subsequent conversations.

62. *Governing California's Coast,* p. xviii.

63. See Willa K. Baum, "Therapeutic Value of Oral History," *International Journal of Aging and Human Development* 12 (1) (1980-81), especially pp. 49-52.

64. See Harriet Zuckerman, "Interviewing an Ultra-Elite," *The Public Opinion Quarterly* 36: 159-175 (1972), 163-164.

65. Ibid., p. 165.

66. Kuhn, director of a project on "Sources for History of Quantum Physics," in a report on August 4, 1964 to Members of the Joint Committee and Other Friends, p. I-II. (Made available to the writer courtesy of Willa K. Baum, Regional Oral History Office of The Bancroft Library.)

67. Sarah Sharp, interviewer/editor at the Regional Oral History Office of The Bancroft Library, in seminar discussion July 8, 1982.

68. The reverse of this process is noted by Lewis Anthony Dexter in a different context—survey research—in a discussion entitled "Toward a Transactional Theory of Interviewing." He noted that a particular writer's work

is valuable because he portrays a situation in which it would have been quite impossible for any interviewer to avoid arousing uncertainties, a sense of being threatened, resentment on the part of some interviewee. (It is interesting that most of the reports on oral history studies do not suggest any experiences as intense.)

One might add further, certainly not as intense, and with any luck, not as disagreeable or even painful. Dexter's comment rings true: uncertainty, threats, resentment, confrontation, hot pursuit, challenge and bluff are equally foreign to the technique of the oral history interview.

See Dexter, *Elite and Specialized Interviewing* (Evanston, Ill.: Northwestern University Press, 1970), p. 151.

69. The use of silence as a manipulative tool in journalistic interviewing provides a revealing contrast. Mary Ellen Leary was reminded of a tactic used by Art Caylor, who wrote a popular column in the *San Francisco News.* She said that Caylor

purposely would go to call on public officials, say "Hello," sit down, and wait! Ask nothing. He found it so unnerved people in public office they'd start tossing him news items—things he didn't know lurked there on their desks so he couldn't have asked about.

One official told me "It was an awful experience. . . . what was he waiting for?" But after a while I learned to have a couple of items, just to keep something on reserve for him." People worked to get him stories, so he'd leave their offices. (Leary, 1984)

70. *Envelopes of Sound,* p. viii.

Chapter V

1. *Reporters' Ethics*, p. 93.

2. See *Problems of Journalism: Proceedings of the 1979 Convention, American Society of Newspaper Editors* (New York, N.Y.: ASNE, 1979), p. 11.

3. Leonard Silk presented the major address at the graduation of Masters of Business Administration candidates from the School of Business Administration, University of California, Berkeley, in the Greek Theater, June 20, 1982.

4. See "U.S. Journalist Accused of Faking Irish Story," by William Tuohy, *Los Angeles Times*, printed in *San Francisco Chronicle*, May 9, 1981, p. 8.

5. Ibid.

6. David Shaw, "More Papers Admitting Their Errors," reprint from the *Los Angeles Times*, Thursday, August 18, 1983, see p. 4 of the reprint.

7. Ibid.

8. David Shaw, "Misleading Headline Stuns N.Y. Times Editor," reprint from the *Los Angeles Times*, dated August 18, 1983, see p. 6 of the reprint.

9. Ibid.

10. See Earl Reeves, "Confrontation in St. Louis," in William L. Rivers, William B. Blankenburg, Kenneth Starck, and Earl Reeves, *Backtalk: Press Councils in America* (San Francisco, Calif: Canfield Press, 1972), pp. 87-107. See p. 100.

11. Some of the most perceptive discussions of reportorial and editorial shortcomings are provided by people in the industry, who are also critics. In a prime example, the *Columbia Journalism Review* presented several articles as "a modest contribution to the discussions that are . . . still going on in newsrooms" with respect to the *Washington Post* story by Janet Cooke that "invented eight-year-old Jimmy the addict, and . . . thereby won and lost a Pulitzer Prize." The introduction stated, "Newspaper hoaxes and the faking of quotes are as old as newspapers themselves." It pointed out that needed changes in coverage are taking place, and that reporters and editors now see their jobs as reporting on "how groups of people. . . . live, and how they feel about their lives. Journalists have become anthropologists." "Exploring Jimmy's World," Comment, *Columbia Journalism Review* 28-36 (July/August 1981), especially p. 28.

12. Fox Butterfield, *Alive in the Bitter Sea* (New York, N.Y.: Times Books, 1982), p. viii.

13. Ibid., p. ix.

14. Tillinghast, *Media Performance*, p. 19.

15. Loc. cit.

16. See "Washington Post admits Pulitzer hoax," *San Francisco Examiner*, April 16, 1981, p. A8.

17. See "Washington Post blames its editors for Pulitzer fiasco," *San Francisco Examiner and Chronicle*, April 19, 1981, p. A6

18. "Another Pulitzer Story Under Fire," *San Francisco Chronicle*, June 12, 1981, p. 7. Criticism by the News Council, which is a "private, independent group. . . . that issues nonbinding decisions on complaints against news organizations."

19. *Reporters' Ethics*, p. 103.

20. Ibid., see p. 50.

21. See "Reporter Faked 'Banzai Run' Story," *San Francisco Chronicle*, September 30, 1981, p. 59.

22. *The Powers That Be*, p. 81.

23. Leary, 1984.

24. Bagdikian, 1984.

25. John Westcott, "To Whom It May Concern" letter received by hand delivery

to the writer, March 31, 1981. Refers to "You Can't Tell the Players Without a Score-card. The 'respectable radicals' and the politics of Berkeley," *California Journal*, April 1981, 143-144.

This story is told in some detail as it developed over a period of several months, and was observed by the writer. As a member of Westcott's Master's Thesis Commit-tee, the writer was favorably impressed with his thesis because it was factually accurate and presented information and analysis of the political situation in a way that seemed fair to both sides. Furthermore, Westcott had done extensive research, and had deepened his knowledge through an internship at the local Berkeley paper, the *Indepen-dent and Gazette.*

In addition, as a subscriber to the *California Journal* since its inception, the writer has found it informative, reliable, and interesting to read, and still does. Salzman's later statement was also candid and helpful.

26. *California Journal*, May 1981, p. 169.

27. The Salzman quotes and comments are from an interview he gave to the writer on January 17, 1984, in Sacramento.

28. See "Top Medical Journals' Bitter Feud Explodes," *San Francisco Chronicle,* January 23, 1981, p. 18. Hereafter "Top Medical Journals' Feud."

29. Arnold S. Relman, "The Ingelfinger Rule," *The New England Journal of Medicine* 305(14): 824-826 (October 1, 1981), p. 824.

30. Ibid., p. 825

31. Loc. cit.

32. "Top Medical Journals' Feud."

33. *Ethics in Social Research,* p. 74.

34. See "Sex researchers criticized for 'flawed' studies," *San Francisco Examiner,* July 29, 1981, p. A5.

Chapter VI

1. See *Changing of the Guard.*

2. William Moss warns that:

In order for the historian to have full confidence in the [oral history inter-view] recording being offered as evidence, he must have a full and authen-ticated record of its creation, preservation, processing, and custody. He needs assurances that the recording was not tampered with, falsified, or edited—or if it was, then by whom, under what circumstances, to what extent, and why?

See Moss, "Oral History: An Appreciation," pp. 87-101, especially p. 95, in David K. Dunaway and Willa K. Baum, eds., *Oral History: An Interdisciplinary Anthology* (Nash-ville, Tenn.: American Association for State and Local History in cooperation with the Oral History Association, 1984). Hereafter, *Oral History.*

3. For a thoughtful discussion of the issue in oral history, see Alice Hoffman, "Reliability and Validity in Oral History," pp. 67-73, in *Oral History.* Hoffman says,

Reliability can be defined as the consistency with which an individual will tell the same story about the same events on a number of different occa-sions. *Validity* refers to the degree of conformity between the reports of the event and the event itself as recorded by other primary resource material such as documents, photographs, diaries, and letters. [emphasis added, see p. 69.]

4. This recognition of the usefulness of interviews does not conflict with a deeply

held view that a journalist's actual presence at meetings of governmental bodies provides better coverage than third-hand accounts or fill. The late Fred Garretson of the *Oakland Tribune* for some time kept a "backside scoreboard" in which he tallied the presence or absence of journalists at meetings such as those of the city council, planning commission, and school board, meetings the journalists covered for their papers. He equated presence at all or most of the meetings with excellence of reporting. The writer also remembers with pleasure the lively and accurate accounts written by Rose Glavinovich and Ed Salzman when they covered the Berkeley City Council meetings in person and often supplemented the stories with interviews.

5. Fosburgh, 1981.

6. See Elizabeth Drew, "Equations," Profile, *New Yorker* 50-129 (May 7, 1979), p. 113.

7. Christopher Evans, *The Mighty Micro: The Impact of the Computer Revolution* (London, England: Victor Gollancz Ltd., 1979), p. 26.

8. Eli Ginsberg, *Good Jobs, Bad Jobs, No Jobs* (Cambridge, Mass.: Harvard University Press, 1979), p. 207.

9. See Dan Bellm, "A Heroine's Story" in the *San Francisco Chronicle Review,* December 22, 1985, pp. 1 and 10, a review of Winnie Mandela, *Part of My Soul Went With Him,* ed. Anne Benjamin; adapted by Mary Benson (New York, N.Y.: W. W. Norton & Co. Inc., 1985).

10. T. Harry Williams, *Huey Long* (New York, N.Y.: Bantam Books, 1970), p. ix.

11. Cyril Birch, Professor, Department of Oriental Languages, UCB, in a discussion of "Writing and Theater in China: Some Current Developments," colloquium, Center for Chinese Studies, UCB, February 27, 1980.

12. *Island,* pp. 8-29, especially pp. 9 and 10. See also "Translation Note," p. 31.

13. Authors Lai and Lim noted that since most of the interviews were conducted in Cantonese, and then translated into English, they retained Cantonese spellings to provide the right flavor for the printed versions.

14. Motives for oral history interviewing can range from preserving family history and anecdotes, folk-wisdom and handcraft methods, to capturing perceptions of elites and leadership groups. Some oral histories are intended to focus on certain realities of life or to reawaken the pride and awareness of groups whose bonds are based, e.g., on ethnic or nationalistic factors, political beliefs, shared experiences, religion, regional or cultural identities, or age.

For an example of "folk history," see William Lynwood Montell, *The Saga of Coe Ridge: A Study in Oral History* (New York, N.Y.: Harper & Row, Harper Torchbooks, 1972); for "life history narratives" of workers, prepared by the Federal Writers Project in the 1930s, see Ann Banks, ed., *First-Person America* (New York, N.Y.: Alfred A. Knopf, 1980); for the lives of aged persons in England, see Ronald Blythe, *The View in Winter: Reflections on Old Age* (New York, N.Y.: Harcourt Brace Jovanovich, 1979). Note that Blythe's sensitive interviews and interpretations are variations on an oral history theme, sharing some characteristics of the technique but retaining the rewriting and interpretation for the interviewer/writer. Paul Thompson, *The Voice of the Past: Oral History* (Oxford, England: Oxford University Press, 1978) is interested in the "relationship between history and the community," and indicated (p. x) that he writes from a socialist perspective. He noted (p. 18) that oral history "allows heroes not just from the leaders, but from the unknown majority of the people. . . . It helps the less privileged, and especially the old, toward dignity and self-confidence." And finally, "It provides a means for a radical transformation of the social meaning of history."

Alistair Horne, in *The New Republic* (March 8, 1980), pp. 33-34, reviewed

Ronald Fraser, *Blood of Spain: An Oral History of the Spanish Civil War* (Pantheon). Horne noted that "Fraser stresses how he largely avoided selecting the top people," but did not give Fraser's reasons. Horne also raised other queries such as "how reliable in general is the technique of oral history—especially when taken down nearly 40 years after the events." The researcher, however could give Fraser high marks for the kind of clarity and candor that warns of the need for factual checking while presenting the "truths" of popular memory.

15. Geoffrey Wigoder, ed., *American Jewish Memoirs: Oral Documentation* (Jerusalem, Israel: Oral History Division, The Institute of Contemporary Jewry, the Hebrew University of Jerusalem, 1980). See pp. 6 and 7.

16. Alex Haley, *Roots* (Garden City, N.Y.: Doubleday & Co., Inc., 1976). Hereafter, *Roots*. See pp. 574, 577, and vii. For a scholarly and somewhat different view of oral tradition, see Jan Vansina, "Oral Tradition and Historical Methodology," pp. 102-106, and Ruth Finnegan, "A Note on Oral Tradition and Historical Evidence," pp. 107-115, in *Oral History*.

17. *Roots,* p. 577.

18. Ibid., p. vii.

19. "To Wake the Dead," Daniel J. Boorstin, *The Discoverers: A History of Man's Search to Know His World and Himself* (New York, N.Y.: Vintage Books, 1985), pp. 588-596. See especially pp. 591-593.

20. Richard Reeves, in *Media Performance,* quotes from pp. 100 and 86 respectively.

21. See "Comment," *Columbia Journalism Review,* January-February 1982, pp. 21-23.

22. Ibid., p. 21.

23. Ibid., p. 23.

24. Ibid., p. 22.

25. Leary, oral history, p. 179.

26. The name of the Teaching Innovation and Evaluation Service was changed in 1985 to Office of Educational Development. The information in this discussion was provided while it was still TIES and uses the original name.

27. Lynn Wood, interview with the writer, November 24, 1981, re. TIES. She also said that the interviewers do not tape-record the interviews because they feel that participants may find tape recorders jarring in the low-key sessions. Further, compared with selective write-ups of "core ideas," interviewers find tapes too costly and time-consuming.

28. Victor Rubin and Elliott A. Medrich, Children's Time Study, UCB School of Law, "After-School Services in a Time of Lowered Expectations: Child Care, Recreation and the Fiscal Crisis," draft paper, 1979.

29. *Phantom Politics.*

30. Leary, *Media Performance,* pp. 1-2.

31. See Harry E. Cross and James A. Sandos, *Across the Border: Rural Development in Mexico and Recent Migration to the United States* (Berkeley, Calif.: Institute of Governmental Studies, University of Caifornia, 1981).

32. *The Best and the Brightest,* see author's note, p. 672.

33. *The Price of Power,* notes: pp. 643-665.

RECENT INSTITUTE PUBLICATIONS

1986

Belzer, Dena and Cynthia Kroll
New Jobs for the Timber Region: Economic Diversification for Northern California. 103pp $6.50

Nathan, Harriet
Critical Choices in Interviews: Conduct, Use, and Research Role. 137pp $5.95

Wilms, Wellford W.
Reshaping Job Training for Economic Productivity (Research Report 86-1). 15pp $3.00

Wyner, Alan J. and Dean E. Mann
Preparing for California's Earthquakes: Local Government and Seismic Safety. 109pp $7.00

1985

Mercer, Lloyd J., W. Douglas Morgan, and Elizabeth Joyce Clingman
California City and County User Charges: Change and Efficiency Since Proposition 13. 101pp $5.25

Stoddart, Trish, David J. Losk, and Charles S. Benson
Some Reflections on the Honorable Profession of Teaching (Research Report 85-1) 35pp $3.50

Willey, Zach
Economic Development and Environmental Quality in California's Water System. 77pp $5.00

Wollenberg, Charles
Golden Gate Metropolis: Perspectives on Bay Area History. 380pp $14.95

1984

Kramer, Ralph and Paul L. Terrell
Social Services Contracting in the San Francisco Bay Area. 42pp $4.00

Leister, Jack, et al., compilers
California Politics and Government, 1970-1983: A Selected Bibliography (Occasional Bibliographies No. 3). 76pp $7.00

Nathan, Harriet and Stanley Scott, eds.
Emerging Issues in Public Policy: Research Reports and Essays, Issues of *Public Affairs Report,* bulletin of the Institute of Governmental Studies, 1977-1982. Four compilations sold separately: Politics, Government, and Related Policy Issues 36pp $2.25; Health and Education 57pp $2.50; Urban Issues, Growth, and the Economy 82pp $3.25; The Environment, Water, and the Coast 108pp $4.00 (Four-volume set $10.00)